NEW AND SELECTED POEMS

NEW and SELECTED POEMS

by KENNETH FEARING

INDIANA UNIVERSITY PRESS · BLOOMINGTON & LONDON

THIRD PRINTING 1974

COPYRIGHT © 1956 BY KENNETH FEARING

LIBRARY OF CONGRESS CATALOG CARD NUMBER: 56-12003

ISBN 0-253-15730-7
MANUFACTURED IN THE UNITED STATES OF AMERICA

Contents

Reading, Writing, and the Rackets

I

THE revolution that calls itself the Investigation had its rise in the theaters of communication, and now regularly parades its images across them, reiterates its gospel from them, daily and hourly marches through the corridors of every office, files into the living-room of every home.

These avenues of communication are television, radio, picture magazines, motion pictures, magazines of news interpretation, digests of news digests, newspaper chains, syndicated features, the house journals of chain industries.

And books. One is apt to overlook that archaic medium. Theoretically, anyone can still write and print a book. But practically, who can announce, distribute, advertise, and secure reviews quite so effectively as the large, economy-package, mail-order book clubs?

In all these forums the Investigation holds court, reveals yesterday's laws, lists the proscribed, debates the dry guillotine to be used next, unveils the confessions rehearsed in its secret trials, proves that its trials are not trials, renews its desperate struggle with those demons that would possess it, specifies those demons for the coming season, then relaxes and performs the cheerier task of erasing memories, of arranging far better horizons for all of us.

The only acts the Investigation does not perform in public are those intimate financial transactions by which each great and little

Investigator reaps the just reward due his superior insight, virtue, and the grave responsibility of exercising so much power. There, the reticence is rarely broken, and then only in moments of awkward, but human, misunderstanding.

Yet that reserve may stem logically enough from a cardinal tenet in the gospel advanced by every tribunal of the Investigation: The need for secrecy is great, and growing.

And here, again, the otherwise bustling and talkative theaters of communication seem to preserve, rather than display, the conduct of those purely private business affairs it might not be in the nation's best interests to know. For the eye can scarcely penetrate beyond the blinding haloes revealed on the electronic screen; the ear catches nothing beneath the repetitions that flow from the loudspeaker; the mind discovers no fresh information between the lines of standard bulletins—all of these in resolute agreement that the circuits of communication defend their freedom and independence of expression, their integrity, against every sinister threat.

So it may well be that there are no financial secrets in the dim, silent region behind the floodlit curtain of public relations, public information, public education, news interpretation, news evaluation, opinion molding, opinion engineering, opinion guidance, fact-finding, and still more public relations.

Surely, if there were a whole industry of chronic largess to conceal—even beneath the haloes—some among these valiant, voluble commentators would ask: Is the richest prize of the Investigation its absolute power to prevent investigation? Is the prolonged public drama of Good v. Evil strictly ersatz, a glittering, noisy substitute for the total darkness, total silence, total secrecy desired?

It is true, such an inquiring reporter would run some risk of personal inconvenience. It might even be suddenly rumored that he has a defect of character, and he might be publicly summoned to a secret examination, or be secretly summoned and put to the question in a public display. Perhaps the Investigation, in its mercy, would return no immediate verdict, at all. Perhaps a subsequent tribunal of the Investigation might reopen the case. Or perhaps not.

In the meantime, though, that reporter could find himself in the limbo of the proscribed.

Still, such an inquisitive and outspoken commentator must exist somewhere, in the giant networks of communication, because so many of its surviving spokesmen, and so many of its freespeech watchmen, tell us so.

But where?

After a decade of victorious inquiries into every agency of communication, conducted in the spotlit arenas of communication, where is the employee who challenges the righteous gospel of the Investigation, slight though its powers may be?

Have you wondered whatever became of the last radio-TV analyst you thought interesting?

"Spies, saboteurs, and traitors" has become a favorite newspaper cliché. In the press of which country is this daily refrain more popular—Russian, or American?

How many societies, legions, councils, and leagues, how many villages and cities, how many departments of city, state, and Federal authorities, now have lists of tabooed books and forbidden authors? Except for press agents of the Investigation, are there any American authors, living or dead, not on one or all of these lists? If you aren't sure about a name or a title, how and where would you inquire, to find out? Or is it safer not to inquire?

And speaking of books—how many books critical of the new gospel have you seen publicly displayed, lately? How many books skeptical of the Investigators' mandate attract favorable comment from the syndicated commentators, or on the cultural forums of the radio-TV hook-ups?

How many of these have there been, lately?

II

Now, there is nothing really new in the foregoing; certainly, not to book readers, who recognize this picture from the most casual acquaintance with history. Rather, it all too clearly resembles those familiar relics with which the deepest and oldest graveyards of the past are filled. And it is not my purpose to detail this giant syndrome that has already made its indelible mark, earning the right to that distinctive name it has chosen for itself: The American Investigation.

But it has a literature peculiar to it, one that is not merely litera-
ture, but also law. This lawgiving literature spells itself out in a
maze of communications that is peculiar to our age, a mechanism
reaching swiftly into the future. These subjects, at least, may be
partly new to the 1956 reader, accustomed chiefly to printed type
and the anachronistic page. Certainly, they are of professional
interest to the 1956 writer, facing the presentation of his work
through a variety of media, both new and old. And facing, of
course, the tribunals of the Investigation, whose legions keep sleep-
less watch upon them all.

By all odds the favorite literary vehicle of the Investigation,
a form now undeniably brought close to perfection, is not without
its prototypes; strictly speaking, its outward design is fairly simple,
one that thirty years ago seemed fully explored, without promise of
further development. (I used to write pieces for the trade, myself;
but I somehow failed to find the revitalizing clue.)

That hardy perennial is the True Confession Story, flourishing
now in the many phases of its amazing renaissance.

The essential ingredients of this narrative form remain about
what they have always been—though today's craftsmanship may
be somewhat superior, perhaps because the rate of pay is higher
and therefore attracts far better talent. (I admit to a certain
amount of envy on this point.) Defining the True Confession
Story, a famed editorial dictum of thirty years ago set down the
law that: "The heroine may fall, but she must *fall upward.*"

This fiat may be a little puzzling today; but in its time, it was
widely and perfectly understood, especially by the writer who had
a True Confession Story in the works. And in contemporary ex-
amples, as we know, the redeemed protagonist must still fall
upward—though how much farther upward, today!

The formula for the True Confession Story, old or new, shows
these abiding features: (1) The Temptation. ("Little did I dream
when the suavely handsome stranger first visited our simple home,
and his glib talk about the glittering life of the underworld set my
pulses racing, that soon this would lead . . .") ("Little did I dream
when my new-found friend, all too aware of my innocence, set
my youthful idealism on fire with his roseate picture of a better
life for the underprivileged, that soon this would lead . . .")

(2) The Fall. In the older True Confession Story, sin was a rather immutable activity, and perhaps for that reason came to seem monotonous. It may be this was where I made my own unfortunate oversight. For while the modern True Confession Story has that frailty, too, it adds others, usually a prolonged adventure in spy work, most often the theft of confidential documents for a foreign power, as for instance the theft of papers that disclose the military secret of garbage. (The reference is literal, in a work that has become a classic.) (3) The Sad Awakening. ("Too late, I realized the cruel deception under that smiling mask, for now the web of trickery I had helped to weave tightened its grip about another victim—myself! Who would believe me, if . . . ?") Such is the melancholy tenor of this turn in the plot-line for both the old and the new type, and it also remains about the same in the conclusion: (4) The Regeneration. ("But come what might, and at whatever cost, I resolved to break with my infamous past and henceforth lead a better life. The break would be irrevocable, and to atone for my past misdeeds I would begin by making a clean breast of everything, I would tell all, including the names. . . .")

Here, of course, there is a sharp divergence between the old, lace-handkerchief type of True Confession Story, and the new, or switchblade type. For the modern variety is strictly utilitarian.

In the past, the literary merits of the True Confession Story, considered as fiction, were dismissed as negligible by those critics most insistent upon the deeper verities of literature. But the contemporary True Confession does not ask to be appraised as fiction. It is presented as fact. And it has the weight of law, with verdict, sentence, and penalty wrapped in one, on the basis that it is fact.

That is the way each succeeding True Confession Story has been acclaimed, as its tale of spies, saboteurs, and traitors emerged from this or that tribunal of the Investigation. As though somehow concerned that their enthusiasm might be doubted, those critics who previously ignored this branch of literature now came to find its revelations not only credible, but possessed of rare insight and literary excellence as well. In radio and television, through daily and hourly reference, each newly sainted author passed at once into the lore of household orthodoxy, while his erstwhile accomplices were accorded a banishment not seen in the centuries since

lepers were belled. The popularity of this latter-day True Con-
fession Story, particularly in legal circles, has been immense, while
the wages of sin, counting book club royalties and motion picture
sales ("at whatever cost"), have been staggering. Indeed, that
critic, book reviewer, editor, or commentator silly enough to carp
at this literary gold rush has almost deserved the obscurity that
suddenly overtook him—provided he did not first experience an
honest, but rapid, change of heart.

There is no record that any of the communications cartels were
reluctant to spread the gospel of the True Confession Story, while
in some of the most public-relations minded, it was a favorite from
the start. In fact, many of the gamier recitals originated within
them, sponsored as the timely Confession of a staff member who
then, in atonement, submitted to the ordeal of royalties and retire-
ment, with honors tactfully bestowed, or of a recently purified spy,
hot from his lurid but underpaid pursuits, employed as an edi-
torial expert to instruct the public, and to aid the tribunals of
the Investigation, in these baffling matters.

For the True Confession Story has always had its practical
advantages. To the question, "Were you, then, a spy, saboteur, and
traitor?" the selected performer gives the acceptable reply, "Yes,
often," and follows this with the useful edge of the pending legis-
lation, "And here are the names of the people and organizations
that aided my espionage. . . ."

This method of persuasion has been so effective that a staff
complement of reformed spies, redeemed saboteurs, regenerate
traitors is deemed to be a living guarantee that the combine is
trustworthy, as the phrase goes, and doubly astute by reason of
former dupedom. Those news services not yet certified with such
consultants, on the other hand, seem hesitant to probe behind the
official bulletins of self-commendation; it is almost as though they
did not desire initiation into the higher probity so certain to follow.
And so the sway of the True Confession Story, throughout the mass
media that nourished it, is absolute.

In our own time, the True Confession also had its public vogue
in Germany and Russia. National pride might urge the boast that
the device is unique with the American Investigation; but perhaps
we can say ours is more democratic.

But what about book writers, theoretically issuing their creative work outside the mills of authoritative information? Poets, novelists, playwrights, none have as yet been accredited to the high-salaried corps of treason and espionage, not even as proscribed runners-up. This may be because we don't have those giant mills of information at our disposal, or in technical terms, don't have any "apparachik." For us, thus far, there are only the auxiliary legions of the Investigation, the book watchers, and a new order they have created for most writers and readers, called dupedom.

Still, even this citation carries penalties, and no profit. It may explain why so many writers have concerned themselves with marginal topics: bold tales of exploration and adventure, heroic stories about the Civil War, amusing anecdotes about one's intrepid (elder) relatives—with anything, in short, save the terrible drama of the past decade, in which a long phase of our society died.

But to understand what has happened to imaginative writing in book form one must realize what is happening now in the matrix of all communications.

III

News, common sense, good literature—these are whatever the voices of communication unanimously, and often, say they are. Conversely, distortion, false reason, base and degenerate writing, these, too, are whatever the concerted organs of communication repeatedly denounce as such. Still more conveniently, those topics and views not mentioned in the forums of communication, at all, do not exist; certainly, if some unpleasant subject does win a momentary, unauthorized interest, under the magic eraser of silence it soon dies.

In the 1956 grid for sending messages to the public, the all-pervasive voice (and face) has long been through the electronic media of radio and television. They have that pre-eminence, and are literally all-pervasive, for they send their messages literally everywhere, send them literally within an instant, and literally permit no rejoinder of either agreement or contradiction.

That the invention of the amplifier means change in every perspective of the writer-audience relationship, far greater and more swiftly than the transformation that followed the invention of movable type, is already too clear to require study. But basic differences between the new and the old media have meaning not generally understood, perhaps because the audience is no more interested in how or why it receives its public messages than it is in what drama, song, or guided tour is on the program of those messages; or perhaps because those who own and direct the printed and the electronic forums see no good reason to dwell upon the differences between them, while there may be many for not doing so.

Some of these differences are plainly lasting, others transient, or recurring. They are:

(1) The direct appeal made to the senses by the electronic media, television particularly, is incomparably more vivid.

(2) The flow of radio-TV presentations is offered essentially free of charge to the audience.

(3) Transmitting apparatus is elaborate and expensive, and a license to broadcast is subject to all the tribunals of the Investigation. There can be no serious invasion by amateurs, here.

(4) The number of transmitters for any given region is further narrowed by today's technological limitations.

(5) Advertising is the business, and the only business, of radio and television. But at its most profitable this goes beyond the simple commercial that extols a product; it offers programs advancing a turn of thought convertible to as much, if not far greater profit. This is propaganda, of course, but in the trade that word has been remodeled to mean a foreign lie, whereas truth, in the trade, is referred to as opinion-molding through public relations. And the basic turn of thought which the juntas of information sell and re-sell is that freedom of expression is the first safeguard of right thinking and right living, a sacred trust of the only (remaining) voices you hear raised, and oddly raised with such identical phrases, in their defense.

(6) The audience does not buy the writer's electronic work. As noted, that is given away free. The work itself is not even offered to the public for sale.

(7) The writer is paid (and very well paid) by the sponsoring

corporation, while he himself has become a corporation writer, one member of a large team that includes an account executive, a station program executive, a network public relations executive, the sponsor's public relations executive, a producer and his human package which includes a director, the starring actor, and two or three other corporation writers who might be called rewrite executives. Several sharp executive heads are better than one, always, and the script that results when all of these free spirits get through subtracting questionable notions from it must be better than just one script written by just one writer, who may know how to spell, but never knows the most important points to be omitted.

(8) The writer has a private name, probably, and he probably has a distinct personality. But his divorce from the transmitted material is complete. That program is the expert salesmanship of another product, not the literary work. And this is a curious reversal of custom that once prevailed in print, and where, even today, there is sometimes a close connection between what a non-corporation writer thinks, and what he writes.

(9) The presentation by air can reach its public instantly, with no time lag unavoidably imposed, as there is in the slower stages of assembling and distributing material in print.

(10) The electronic program is presented but once. Only singing commercials, and favorite texts from official True Confession stories, are authentic classics of our age, apparently, and merit so many repeat performances, such frequent references.

(11) Once transmitted, the electronic message is gone forever, and for most of its audience, gone beyond recall.

(12) Nor does the message leave a public record of itself. The tape and film of its most dramatic hours, its most casual—or critical—months and years cannot be found in any public library. They may exist, briefly, in private files. But there is nowhere a catalogue (nor even an effective method for cataloguing) clues to identify the nature of the electronic past. In these media, today's mesage is always authentic; it is permanently the very latest word, of course, but it is more. Because it can never be confronted with a previous message that might contain material to contradict it, it is also the first word, and the only word. And the same message, daily repeated, always a self-declared corroboration of itself, can also

be slightly altered from day to day, be given a steadily changing perspective, can remain forever the same message, and yet not be remotely the same at all.

The swarming of the Investigators coincided exactly, in time, with the swift development of television.

In all media of communication the larger syndicates welcomed and helped formulate the structure, the menacing techniques of the Investigation, though resistance flickered briefly in isolated pockets of the press. But that separate enclosure in the world of communications, television, quickly joined by radio, has never had a station, or even a spokesman, independent of the opinion-molders who, since they also mold the law, are in effect our official bureaus of information. The governors of electronics do not talk much about the kinds of power inherent in the form, save skimpily as "a force for public service;" they do not even openly analyze foreign use of electronic control; the study could not fail to suggest parallels. But it seems most probable that, in spite of the usual bizarre and ambitious plans that have certainly been laid, no unified program exists. The medium is really new, and in electronic communication, the year is once more 1450.

Yet it is today the determinant in all other circuits of communication, on policies of acceptable and inacceptable thought. Repetition, with no standard for comparison, is the basic and invincible logic of the screen, the loudspeaker; with timely repetition, their spokesmen gild and regild the lily. Sentimental souls who attach mystic powers to the printed word have not yet reflected that among the new recruits of today's generation, one of them will read, to a hundred who become auditors, only, and that tomorrow the ratio will be one to a thousand.

Inside the electronic world, the screening and control of public messages occurs at the many check-points previously noted, and there is little need for the blunt intervention of archaic censorship (though no doubt it is sometimes exercised, without any audience learning, or much caring, that it has taken place). But most of the control is automatic. Instead of blue-penciling passages suspect of sinister intent, it is easier to cancel the commentator or executive sub-editor who tends to be careless about the by-laws governing free speech. New and younger editors invariably function better; they have no illegal information, no haunting memories to forget.

And in those cartels of communication outside of electronics, opposition, or even a strongly divergent vogue, runs the risk of the familiar, devious contest it cannot win. For the airborne legions can be marshaled instantly and concentrated anywhere, unleashed in any degree of the expert ferocity we have so often seen in the past decade—always as a public service, with the classic seal of divine authority, as well.

But even the suggestion of discord between the electronic world and the satellite press seems monstrous. All time and all space in every medium is merchandise, so expensive and so profitable in the great treasure hunt of the day that not a moment, not a line can be wasted on matters irrelevant to communications as a flourishing commerce. What other, better kind of freespeech can there possibly be than news and opinion that pays such dividends?

IV

APPROVED rhetoric in 1956 seems an innocent recital of endless prosperity, occasionally interspersed with grim but imperative demonstrations against super-demons that endanger this idyl. There is very little in the flow of simplified bulletins that would move anyone to second, longer thoughts. The artless messages are uniform. There can be no surprises in them, for they use the language of subtraction, from which every discordant thought and detail has been skilfully pared and removed.

But the recital seems less innocent, when the prolonged hammering and grinding by which it has been processed is reviewed. What has been removed (not counting a few human heads) to produce this loss-proof package, and what ersatz filler has been added to replace the subtracted matter? And then, this industry is not merely one more among many; it is the central nervous system that actuates, or paralyzes, a whole society. There can be nothing artless about the control of a mechanism so powerful; a simplified ideological jargon cannot be the practical key to the source and disposition of a wealth so vast. We know, too well, the log cabins and covered wagons processed by the opinion-molding settlements of Madison and Pennsylvania Avenues, and we are equally familiar with the host of spies, saboteurs, and traitors besieging them; but we do not hear, save inferentially, about the loot, pillage, and plunder inseparable from absolute power exercised in, and through, the networks of communication, captive and menaced as they all are.

The character and volume of this under-the-counter commerce today, in terms of cash rather than the exalted international and supernatural labels exhibited, can only be surmised, and then only by comparison with the last, similarly prosperous, similarly secretive epoch in our history for which there is even a partially established record. That was the age dedicated, outwardly, to Prohibition; more privately, it marked this society's first, universal introduction to the uses of Protection, blazing trails to new careers, founding new dynasties, pioneering an entire continent for the code and practice of the rackets. The press of that age was not thoroughly homogenized, and some sense of the splendid business opportunities offered in the link between Prohibition and Protection eventually became public knowledge. There is no evidence that these silent transactions have at any time been seriously inconvenienced since that wholesale prelude.

Today, little issues from the public address system of communications other than sponsored salesmanship, filled with the easier types of true thoughts, but wholly pruned of thoughts everyone knows are false; and of course, the verdicts of the Security courts, maintaining freedom. A visiting de Tocqueville might marvel that so much of the national wealth is channeled into social and military insurance against the stern needs of the future, at the same time supporting such visible prosperity in the present; that foreign visitor might be entranced at the way these riches are administered with a log-cabin virtue questioned by absolutely none. But not many of us are innocents from abroad. The signs, the classic situations, the covering language designed for an adult kindergarten are too familiar; this looks like a society necrobiotic with the rackets.

It would be pointless, and certainly thankless, to speculate which has been imposed on the other, the native rackets, or the common Twentieth-century plague. Perhaps these are identical, and always have been. It is a world that does not really need a scale of values; money is better. But a rudimentary cover-up can be a help, and the grandiose pitch for it is summed up in the True Confession Story. An orderly inversion of reason is the operative principle, and with this key the outcome of impending trials and issues can be foreseen in their earliest notices. Thus, race murder in a backward area is officially declared a mirage (it didn't happen) perpetrated (on a nameless stranger, to create false sympathy) by the victim's accomplices, who are spies, saboteurs, traitors, dupes, and this decree must pass with no question from the public message carriers, since it is the grotesque essence of the True Confession Story the communications circuits enforce everywhere. And so, too, the strategists of the Investigation are forever "losing" in the unequal contest to save us from dire peril, enfeebled and helpless as they have been since their earliest triumphs. Now, whenever that forlorn cry is raised it constitutes the sole announcement that another social domain has been invaded and sacked. Courage, similarly, is an attribute that has undergone a curious change in the scale of this new regime. It is now the valor of a freshly persuaded witness before the Investigation, recklessly defying the demons of spydom, protected only by all the organized forces of a once powerful nation that emerged victorious—before the rise of the Investigation—from a global war.

It should be apparent that creative writers, those not primarily moved to produce commercially acceptable copy, will find it paralyzing to work within the purposeful, voracious, medieval terms of the official code. (Though the television networks, as everyone knows, produce dramas that daily surpass themselves; they say so.) And it should also be apparent that there is no province of communication immune to the blackdamp of these authorized values. The proprietors of the new order intend to obliterate avenues of the imagination they cannot sanctify, including further plans for the world of books.

V

READING is one form of education, but writing seems to have educational by-products and after-effects that come in all forms. Some of these experiences that at least feel the most broadening are not, of course, deliberately invited. A zest for knowledge and self-improvement did not loom very large as a motive in my first subscription to the literary life, I imagine; what I had in mind, I'm sure, was some fascinating way to be of public service, particularly one that avoided too much humdrum routine in an office cluttered with, well, books.

There can be a unique exhilaration in creative writing, and it can offer the surprise of final discovery. These qualities exist in life (sometimes), and if they are not to be found in a verbal presentation of it, then the reader (or audience) has been cheated and the writer has been killing everyone's time. This excitement and surprise must be real, not counterfeit, and have in it the breath of those crises upon which most people feel their lives are poised, sometimes crossing into them, in fact, and then rarely with routine behavior, seldom with standardized results. A writer cannot do much to transmit an excitement he does not feel, and the only surprises are those that find themselves, as the work grows. None of these essentials that fuse hard uncertainty, tension, choice, and action into a sense of reality are possible, working inside the cartels of communication. The technique of subtraction, which means such rich dividends to a public relations firm, is also total bankruptcy to the creative imagination. These limitations have always held, of course, in the largest media; they are not established by the new mechanical devices for presentation, which have dazzling possibilities; they arise from the purposes for which they are controlled, and the flowering of the rackets merely added virulence to the original stagnation. Since that flowering, all literary work has grown steadily safer, risk-proofed against steadily multiplying taboos.

As an escape from routine, therefore, my choice of an activity related to communications would seem to be about the worst possible. But the margin by which inventive writing is separated from the Executive Story Conference imitation of it has not always been a desolate no man's land patrolled by reformed spies, saboteurs, traitors, monitored by converted Russian Intelligence officers and cultured plantation owners, booby-trapped with amendments to the Constitution. Before the eclipse, there was some barter, and human communication was quite possible without character references from these new literary arbiters. Commercial scripts must always be exactly the same, but different, and in their feverish search for a totally different sameness, story executives chronically send for another, far better, far more sensible imaginative writer, and he, in turn, needs money.

These collisions have been educational, and sometimes they have even been fun. They have been a direct source of material, too. I see that I attended a story conference in 1940, or a little before, and in the course of it we faithfully performed all the steps of subtraction necessary to make some heartbreak series exactly the same as the cycle that preceded it. The poem "Yes, the Agency Can Handle That" attempts to dramatize the process of the story conference in which, I suppose, two or three executives, probably with my help, beat every last shred of plausibility out of one of those moving, true-to-life sagas. I was rather gloomily fascinated by the skill and care taken to weed out every possible sales deterrent, and so I wrote about it. Then a few years later, I drew on a segment of communications for the setting of a novel, *The Big Clock*. The rigor mortis overtaking that mythical nerve center was a little too educational; "Anything but the News" was some character's facetious description of its published output; but the cream of the joke was far more grisly, for soon the ersatz issued by all such gazettes would fill with spy recitals, as the great treasure hunt gathered momentum; it was the eve of the first *coups* staged by the Americaneers in and with a world of communications already moribund.

To write about the people and events of this time and this place, through imaginary characters and transposed circumstances, all of it coming in the end to an expression of the changing relationships between people in varied crises—this has not always been an unmixed pleasure, of course. Some of the evidence has been too conclusive and too appalling, even for me. And it has been a privilege (though I can think of safer ones) to learn something of the nature of the eclipse, and to know people better in the way they met it, chiefly through the discipline enforced by writing about them in the margin of whatever light remained.

But there are other forms of crisis on everyone's private,

crowded calendar, apart from the central tragedy; other moods, other people, or the same people in different circumstances. Technically speaking, the mood in which a work is presented is probably the largest factor in the effect it makes; it's invisible, since it can't be pointed out, but it's there; essentially, it's the relationship established between the author and the reader, during the course of a conversation in which the author does all the talking. In poetry, the tone establishes the rhythm, which is literally the sound of that conversation, and carries just about all the meaning of the poem.

These poems were written in a variety of moods, not intentionally so, with a view to filling prescriptions, but because at one time or another I felt that way. Never, though, merely because I thought that way. And in this collection, only a small fraction of the poems relate directly to the corrosion outlined in preceding sections of this foreword. If I had already covered that subject, there would have been no urge to work with the same gruesome material again. Most of these poems are keyed to other moods, and while I never made an absolute requirement of this, it has always been a thought that each poem was in a different vein from all the others.

KENNETH FEARING

New York City, April, 1956

NEW AND SELECTED POEMS

ST. AGNES' EVE

The settings include a fly-specked Monday evening,
A cigar store with stagnant windows,
Two crooked streets;
The characters: six policemen and Louie Glatz.

Subways rumble and mutter a remote portent
As Louie Glatz holds up the cigar store and backs out with

$14.92.

Officer Dolan noticed something suspicious, it is supposed,
And ordered him to halt,
But dangerous, handsome, cross-eyed Louie the rat

Spoke with his gat
Rat-a-tat-tat
Rat-a-tat-tat
And Dolan was buried as quickly as possible.

But Louie didn't give a good God damn,
He ran like a crazy shadow on a shadowy street,
With five policemen called to that beat
Hot on his trail, going Blam! Blam! Blam!

While rat-a-tat-tat
Rat-a-tat-tat
Said Louie's gat,

So loud that Peter Wendotti rolled away from his wife,
Got out of bed to scratch his stomach and shiver on the cold floor
Listening to the stammering syllables of instant death met on
    secret floors in the big vacant galleries of night.

Then Louie sagged and fell and ran.
With seven bullets through his caved-in skull and those feeble
       brains spilling out like soup,
He crawled behind a water hydrant and stood them off for an-
       other half minute.

"I'm not shot," he yelled. "I'm not shot," he screamed. "It isn't
       me they've shot in the head," he laughed. "Oh,
I don't give a damn!"

And rat-a-tat-tat
Rat-a-tat-tat
Stuttered the gat
Of Louie the rat,
While the officers of the law went Blam! Blam! Blam!

Soft music, as the wind moans at curtained windows and shut-
       tered doors.
The vibrant throats of steamships hoot a sad defiance at distance
       and nothing.
Space lays its arm across the flat roofs and dreary streets.
Bricks bulge and sag.

Louie's soul arose through his mouth in the form of a derby hat
       that danced with cigarette butts and burned matches and
       specks of dust where Louie sprawled.
Close-up of Dolan's widow. Of Louie's mother.
Picture of the fly-specked Monday evening, and fade out slow.

2

MINNIE AND MRS. HOYNE

She could die laughing,
On Sunday noon, back of the pawnshop, under the smoke-stack,
    with Mrs. Hoyne.
She could hide her face in rags and die laughing on the street.
She could snicker in the broom closet. In the dark of the movies.
    In bed.

Die, at the way some people talk.
The things they talk about and believe and do.
She and Mrs. Hoyne could sit together and laugh.
Minnie could snicker in the dark alone.

Jesus, what do they mean?
Girls trying to be in love.
People worried about other people. About the world. Do they
    own it?
People that don't believe a street is what it looks like. They think
    there's more.
There isn't any more, the cuckoos.
She could die laughing.
Free milk for babies, Mrs. Hoyne.

Crazy liars, all of them, and what next?
Minnie will be a millionaire.
Mrs. Hoyne will fly a balloon.
Give my regards to the Queen of France when you get there.
Ask her if she remembers me. "Say, Queen, have you got any old
    bloomers you don't want, for Minnie Spohr?"
She could die, grinning among the buckets at midnight,
Snicker, staring down the elevator shaft,
Minnie doesn't care. Get the money, that's all.
She could die laughing, some time,
Alone in the broom closet among the mops and brushes on the
    forty-third floor.

ANDY AND JERRY AND JOE

We were staring at the bottles in the restaurant window,
We could hear the autos go by,
We were looking at the women on the boulevard,
It was cold,
No one else knew about the things we knew.

We watched the crowd, there was a murder in the papers, the
     wind blew hard, it was dark,
We didn't know what to do,
There was no place to go and we had nothing to say,
We listened to the bells, and voices, and whistles, and cars,
We moved on,
We weren't dull, or wise, or afraid,
We didn't feel tired, or restless, or happy, or sad.

There were a million stars, a million miles, a million people, a
     million words,
A million places and a million years,
We knew a lot of things we could hardly understand.
There were liners at sea, and rows of houses here, and clouds that
     floated past us away up in the sky.
We waited on the corner,
The lights were in the stores, there were women on the streets,
     Jerry's father was dead,
We didn't know what we wanted and there was nothing to say,
Andy had an auto and Joe had a girl.

JOHN STANDISH, ARTIST

If I am to live, or be in the studios,
If I am to be in the quiet halls and clubs,
Quiet at tea,
If I am to talk calmly at dinner, when evening falls,
If I am to breathe—

When it is night, and millions are awake, moving like a sea, not
     human, not known,
When millions are aroused to stare, to laugh, to kill,
When I feel them,
When they have no voices, but they have mouths and eyes,
When their wants are confused, but implacable,
When a theory about them becomes nothing, and a portrait of
     them would look well on no studio wall,
When they cringe, when they scowl, when they are counted by
     millions,
When they have no meaning to me, to themselves, to the earth,
     but they are alive—

If I am to live, if I am to breathe,
I must walk with them a while, laugh with them, stare and point,
Pick one and follow him to the rotted wharves,
Write my name, under his, in gray latrines, "John Standish, artist,"
I must follow him, stumbling as he does, through the docks, base-
     ments, tenements, wharves,
Follow him till he sleeps, and kill him with a stone.

Professor Burke's symphony, "Colorado Vistas,"
In four movements,
I Mountains, II Canyons, III Dusk, IV Dawn,
Was played recently by the Philharmonic.
Snapshots of the localities described in music were passed around
and the audience checked for accuracy.
All O.K.
After the performance Maurice Epstein, 29, tuberculosis, stoker on
the S.S. *Tarboy*, rose to his feet and shouted,
"He's crazy, them artists are all crazy,
I can prove it by Max Nordau. They poison the minds of young
girls."
Otto Svoboda, 500 Avenue A, butcher, Pole, husband, philosopher,
argued in rebuttal,
"Shut your trap, you.
The question is, does the symphony fit in with Karl Marx?"

At the Friday evening meeting of the Browning Writing League,
Mrs. Whittamore Ralston-Beckett,
Traveler, lecturer, novelist, critic, poet, playwright, editor, mother,
idealist,
Fascinated her audience with a brief talk, whimsical and caustic,
Appealing to the younger generation to take a brighter, happier,
more sunny and less morbid view of life's eternal funda-
mentals.
Mrs. Ralston-Beckett quoted Sir Henry Parke-Bennett: "O
Beauty," she said,
"Take your fingers off my throat, take your elbow out of my eye,
Take your sorrow off my sorrow,
Take your hat, take your gloves, take your feet down off the table,
Take your beauty off my beauty, and go."

In the open discussion that followed, Maurice Epstein, 29, tuber-
culosis, stoker on the S. S. *Tarboy*, arose and queried the
speaker,

"Is it true, as certain scientists assert, that them artists are all of
them crazy?"
A Mr. Otto Svoboda present spoke in reply,
"Shut your trap, you. The question is, what about Karl Marx?"

"Myrtle loves Harry"—It is sometimes hard to remember a thing
     like that,
Hard to think about it, and no one knows what to do with it when
     he has it,
So write it out on a billboard that stands under the yellow light
     of an "L" platform among popcorn wrappers and crushed
     cigars,
A poster that says "Mama I Love Crispy Wafers So."
Leave it on a placard where somebody else gave the blonde lady a
     pencil moustache, and another perplexed citizen deposited:
"Jesus Saves. Jesus Saves."
One can lay this bundle down there with the others,
And never lose it, or forget it, or want it.
"Myrtle loves Harry."
They live somewhere.

NOW

Now that we know life:
Breakfast in the morning; office and theater and sleep; no memory;
Only desire and profit are real;
Now that we know life in our own way,

There is no war, no death,
There are no doubts, no terrors, and we make no mistakes;
There is a forest of bones in the earth but above it, now there is
      peace;
The fury is gone;
The purposes are gone;
For a little while, the agony is gone;
We have our own thoughts, we know life in our own way,
The world is quiet and green—

As it is where bubbles rise in the waters of swamps;
Where bubbles of gas rise and break among the reeds;
And the reeds are green;
And the frogs are loud, the water is warm where the bubbles rise;
The reeds are still;
The reeds are green, the water is warm, the sky is blue.

GREEN LIGHT

Bought at the drug store, very cheap; and later pawned.
After a while, heard on the street; seen in the park.
Familiar, but not quite recognized.
Followed and taken home and slept with.
Traded or sold. Or lost.

Bought again at the corner drug store,
At the green light, at the patient's demand, at nine o'clock.
Re-read and memorized and re-wound.
Found unsuitable.
Smashed, put together, and pawned.

Heard on the street, seen in a dream, heard in the park, seen by
      the light of day;
Carefully observed one night by a secret agent of the Greek Hy-
      draulic Mining Commission, in plain clothes, off duty.
The agent, in broken English, took copious notes. Which he lost.
Strange, and yet not extraordinary.
Sad, but true.

True, or exaggerated, or true;
As it is true that the people laugh and the sparrows fly;
As it is exaggerated that the people change, and the sea stays;
As it is that the people go;
As the lights go on and it is night and it is serious, and just the
      same;
As some one dies and it is serious, and the same;
As a girl knows and it is small, and true;
As the corner hardware clerk might know and it is true, and
      pointless;
As an old man knows and it is grotesque, but true;
As the people laugh, as the people think, as the people change,
It is serious and the same, exaggerated or true.

Bought at the drug store down the street
Where the wind blows and the motors go by and it is always night,
       or day;
Bought to use as a last resort,
Bought to impress the statuary in the park.
Bought at a cut rate, at the green light, at nine o'clock.
Borrowed or bought. To look well. To ennoble. To prevent disease.
       To entertain. To have.
Broken or sold. Or given away. Or used and forgotten. Or lost.

INVITATION

We will make love, when the hospitals are quiet and the blue
  police car stops to unload prisoners,
We will sleep, while the searchlights go across the sky,
We will dine, while the destitute actor shakes hands cordially
  in an uptown bar,
We will be alone, we will go to the theater, we will be drunk,
  perhaps we shall die, and there will be a thousand lovers
  on the bus-tops, they will find the suicide lying on the
  floor of a furnished room.

It will be morning when the old men are dreaming again in sunlit
  parks,
It will be night when the movie heroine smiles once more through
  perfect tears,
Night when the bank cashier is blackmailed and crowds are mut-
  tering in the square, night when a girl walks with head
  turned back to watch the shadows following through dim
  streets,
It will be night when the judge drinks with the salesman and the
  lady novelist bares her soul,
Night when we laugh,
It will be night when pleasure turns to agony, agony to terror, ter-
  ror to rage, rage to delight,
It will be morning when we forget,
It will be morning when the air grows warm, and we read the
  news.

Here we will be invited by thundering feet, desolate faces, laugh-
  ter, cunning eyes, eyes bright with love, lips tightened
  in pain,
Here we will be urged by reality confused with dream,
We will be urged by the hunger of the live, trapped by the relent-
  less purposes of millions,
With the millions we will know this, and we will forget,
We will be aroused, we will make love, we will dream, we will
  travel through endless spaces, and we will smile across
  the room.

12

CONCLUSION

You will give praise to all things, praise without end;
Idly in the morning, bluntly at noon, cunningly with the evening
    cigar, you will meditate further praise;
So will the days pass, each profitable and serene; so will your sleep
    be undisturbed; so you will live;
No faith will be difficult, rising from doubt; no love will be false,
    born of dread;

In the flaring parks, in the taverns, in the hushed academies, your
    murmur will applaud the wisdom of a thousand quacks.
    For theirs is the kingdom.
By your sedate nod in the quiet office you will grieve with the
    magnate as he speaks of sacrifice. For his is the power.
Your knowing glance will affirm the shrewd virtue of clown and
    drudge; directors' room or street-corner, the routine killer
    will know your candid smile; your handclasp, after the
    speeches at the club, will endorse the valor of loud sub-
    urban heroes. For theirs is the glory, forever and ever.

Always, more than wise, you will be found with the many resolved
    against the few;
But you will be a brother, on second thought, to all men.

The metropolitan dive, jammed with your colleagues, the dere-
    licts; the skyscraper, owned by your twin, the pimp of
    gumdrops and philanthropy; the auditoriums, packed with
    weeping creditors, your peers; the morgues, tenanted by
    your friends, the free dead; the asylums, cathedrals, prisons,
    treasuries, brothels, shrines—upon all, all of them you will
    find reason to bestow praise;

And as you know, at last, that all of this will be,
As you walk among millions, indifferent to them,
Or stop and read the journals filled with studied alarm,
Or pause and hear, with no concern, the statesman vending manu-
    factured bliss,

13

You will be grateful for an easy death,
Your silence will praise them for killing you.

WINNER TAKE ALL

Innocent of the mean or stupid, and innocent of crime,
Still, justice denied you, from this extremity there is no escape.

Say to the accusing eyes, say to the doctor standing at your death-
      bed, say to the memory of your mistakes, say you are
      innocent,
Say to the telegram announcing death you are innocent of death,
Say to the ticker that wipes you out this failure was not to be fore-
      seen,

Tell the black headlines, shouting your infamy to millions, that
      even a judge has to have what he has to have
(And they say you've been bought, fixed, call it a bribe when you
      borrow money from a friend).

Yes, tell the neighbors,
After he's gone, calling you a lowdown doublecrossing tramp,
Tell them you are innocent
(A woman's got to have what she's got to have, and you had to
      have that man).

Say to the world you are a man to be valued, beyond the reach of
      brisk refusal and command,
Say you are a gentleman, untouched by the pettiness forced upon
      you,
Say you, also, are a motion-picture queen, innocent of vacant
      nights, useless desires, bargain heroes,

Go on, tell the jury you are innocent of murder
(Shooting at an arm reaching for a gun to drop you dead),
Robbery, yes, but you never meant to kill that crazy fool, yes,
      robbery,
But who knows how you needed money?—

You've got to have what you've got to have, you're going to do
    what you've got to do,
And you are innocent of what has to happen,
Innocent, when they put you out on the street, when they look
    at you and laugh, when you grow old and fade away, when
    they strap you in the electric chair,
Tell them all you are innocent, innocent of this.

What if they don't listen, and there is no escape?
Still you are innocent, and brave, and wise, and strong.

RESURRECTION

You will remember the kisses, real or imagined;
You will remember the faces that were before you, and the words
    exchanged;
You will remember the minute crowded with meaning, the mo-
    ment of pain, the aimless hour;
You will remember the cities, and the plains, and the mountains,
    and the sea,

And recall the friendly voice of the killer, or the voice of the priest,
    inhumanly sweet;
Recall the triumphant smile of the duped;
You will not forget compassion that glittered in the eyes of the
    money-lender, refusing you, not forget the purpose that lay
    beneath the merchant's warmth;
You will not forget the voice of the bought magistrate quivering in
    horror through the courtroom above prostitute and pimp,
The majesty of the statesman at the microphone, the sober majesty
    of the listening clerk,
The face of the fool, radiant on newspaper and screen;

You will remember hope that crawled up the bar-room tap and
    spoke through the confident speech of the lost,
Happiness clearly displayed on the glaring billboards,
Love casually revealed in the magazines and novels, or stated in
    the trembling limbs of ancient millionaires;
You will remember the triumph easily defined by the rebel mes-
    siah, by the breadloaf in the hand of the ghetto wife, by the
    inscription on the patriot tomb;
You will remember your laughter that rose with the steam from
    the carcass on the street
In hatred and pity exactly matched.

These are the things that will return to you,
To mingle with the days and nights, with the sound of motors and
    the sun's warmth,

With fatigue and desire,
As you work, and sleep, and talk, and laugh, and die.

OBITUARY

Take him away, he's as dead as they die,
Hear that ambulance bell, his eyes are staring straight at death;
Look at the fingers growing stiff, touch the face already cold, see
　　the stars in the sky, look at the stains on the street,

Look at the ten-ton truck that came rolling along fast and
　　stretched him out cold,

Then turn out his pockets and make the crowd move on.
Sergeant, what was his name? What's the driver's name? What's
　　your name, sergeant?
Go through his clothes,
Take out the cigars, the money, the papers, the keys, take every-
　　thing there is,

And give a dollar and a half to the Standard Oil. It was his true-
　　blue friend.
Give the key of his flat to the D.A.R. They were friends of his, the
　　best a man ever had.
Take out the pawnticket, wrap it, seal it, send it along to the
　　People's Gas. They were life-long pals. It was more than
　　his brother. They were just like twins.

Give away the shoes,
Give his derby away. Donate his socks to the Guggenheim fund,
Let the Morgans hold the priceless bills, and leaflets, and racing
　　tips under lock and key,
And give Mr. Hoover the pint of gin,
Because they're all good men. And they were friends of his.

Don't forget Gene Tunney. Don't forget Will Hays. Don't forget
　　Al Capone. Don't forget the I.R.T.
Give them his matches to remember him by.
They lived with him, in the same old world. And they're good
　　men, too.

19

That's all, sergeant. There's nothing else, lieutenant. There's no
     more, captain.
Pick up the body, feed it, shave it, find it another job.

Have a cigar, driver?
Take two cigars—
You were his true-blue pal.

DIVIDENDS

This advantage to be seized; and here, an escape prepared against
    an evil day;
So it is arranged, consummately, to meet the issues. Convenience
    and order. Necessary murder and divorce. A decent repute.

Such are the plans, in clear detail.
She thought it was too soon but they said no, it was too late. They
    didn't trust the other people.
Sell now.
He was a fool to ignore the market. It could be explained, he said.
    With the woman, and after the theater she made a scene.
    None of them felt the crash for a long time.

(But what is swifter than time?)

So it is resolved, upon awakening. This way it is devised, prepar-
    ing for sleep. So it is revealed, uneasily, in strange dreams.
A defense against gray, hungry, envious millions. A veiled watch
    to be kept upon this friend.
Dread that handclasp. Seek this one. Smile.
They didn't trust the others. They were wary. It looked suspicious.
    They preferred to wait, they said.

Gentlemen, here is a statement for the third month,
And here, Mildred, is the easiest way.
Such is the evidence, convertible to profit. These are the divi-
    dends, waiting to be used.
Here are the demands again, considered again, and again the end-
    less issues are all secure.
Such are the facts. Such are the details. Such are the proofs.

Almighty God, these are the plans,
These are the plans until the last moment of the last hour of the
    last day,

And then the end. By error or accident.
Burke of cancer. Jackson out at the secret meeting of the board.
      Hendricks through the window of the nineteenth floor.
Maggots and darkness will attend the alibi.

Peace on earth. And the finer things.
So it is all devised.
Thomas, the car.

X MINUS X

Even when your friend, the radio, is still; even when her dream,
      the magazine, is finished; even when his life, the ticker, is
      silent; even when their destiny, the boulevard, is bare;
And after that paradise, the dance-hall, is closed; after that the-
      ater, the clinic, is dark,

Still there will be your desire, and hers, and his hopes and theirs,
Your laughter, their laughter,
Your curse and his curse, her reward and their reward, their
      dismay and his dismay and her dismay and yours—

Even when your enemy, the collector, is dead; even when your
      counsellor, the salesman, is sleeping; even when your
      sweetheart, the movie queen, has spoken; even when your
      friend, the magnate, is gone.

What will you do when the phone rings and they say to you:
What will you do?

What will you say, when the sun lights all the avenue again,
and the battle monument still reads: These dead did not
die in vain?

When night returns, when the clock strikes one, the clock strikes
two, three, four, when the city sleeps, awakes, when day
returns, what will you say, feel, believe, do,

Do with the culture found in a tabloid, what can be done with
a Lydia Pinkham ad?

What reply can you give to the pawnclerk's decent bid for your
silverware?

How are you to be grateful as "Thrift" glares out, in a hundred
thousand watts, across the ghetto nights; reassured, as the
legless, sightless one extends his cup; who can be surprised,
why, how, as the statesman speaks for peace and moves
for war?

Then, when they tell you the executioner does the best that he
can, what can you say? What then?

Or they come to you, as human fingers comb the city's refuse, and
say, Look, you have been saved;

When they tell you: See, you were right, and it is the day the
utilities evidence has been destroyed;

And the state is saved again (three dead, six shot), and they tell
you, Look, you have survived, the reward is yours, you
have won—What then? What then?

What will you say and where will you turn?
What will you do? What will you do? What will you do?

Whether dinner was pleasant, with the windows lit by gunfire,
and no one disagreed; or whether, later, we argued in the
park, and there was a touch of vomit-gas in the evening air;

Whether we found a greater, deeper, more perfect love, by
courtesy of Camels, over NBC; whether the comics amused
us, or the newspapers carried a hunger death and a White
House prayer for Mother's Day;

Whether the bills were paid or not, whether or not we had our
doubts, whether we spoke our minds at Joe's, and the
receipt said "Not Returnable," and the cash-register rang
up "No Sale,"

Whether the truth was then, or later, or whether the best had
already gone—

Nevertheless, we know; as every turn is measured; as every un-
avoidable risk is known;

As nevertheless, the flesh grows old, dies, dies in its only life, is
gone;

The reflection goes from the mirror; as the shadow, of even a
rebel, is gone from the wall;

As nevertheless, the current is thrown and the wheels revolve; and
nevertheless, as the word is spoken and the wheat grows
tall and the ships sail on—

None but the fool is paid in full; none but the broker, none but
the scab is certain of profit;

The sheriff alone may attend a third degree in formal attire;
alone, the academy artists multiply in dignity as trooper's
bayonet guards the door;

Only Steve, the side-show robot, knows content; only Steve, the
mechanical man in love with a photo-electric beam, re-
mains aloof; only Steve, who sits and smokes or stands in
salute, is secure;

Steve, whose shoebutton eyes are blind to terror, whose painted ears are deaf to appeal, whose welded breast will never be slashed by bullets, whose armature soul can hold no fear.

DIRGE

1-2-3 was the number he played but today the number came 3-2-1;
Bought his Carbide at 30 and it went to 29; had the favorite at
    Bowie but the track was slow—

O executive type, would you like to drive a floating-power, knee-
    action, silk-upholstered six? Wed a Hollywood star? Shoot
    the course in 58? Draw to the ace, king, jack?
O fellow with a will who won't take no, watch out for three
    cigarettes on the same, single match; O democratic voter
    born in August under Mars, beware of liquidated rails—

Denouement to denouement, he took a personal pride in the cer-
    tain, certain way he lived his own, private life,
But nevertheless, they shut off his gas; nevertheless, the bank fore-
    closed; nevertheless, the landlord called; nevertheless, the
    radio broke,

And twelve o'clock arrived just once too often,
Just the same he wore one gray tweed suit, bought one straw hat,
    drank one straight Scotch, walked one short step, took one
    long look, drew one deep breath,
Just one too many,

And wow he died as wow he lived,
Going whop to the office and blooie home to sleep and biff got
    married and bam had children and oof got fired,
Zowie did he live and zowie did he die,

With who the hell are you at the corner of his casket, and where
    the hell're we going on the right-hand silver knob, and who
    the hell cares walking second from the end with an Amer-
    ican Beauty wreath from why the hell not,

Very much missed by the circulation staff of the New York Eve-
    ning Post; deeply, deeply mourned by the B.M.T.

27

Wham, Mr. Roosevelt; pow, Sears Roebuck; awk, big dipper;
   bop, summer rain;
Bong, Mr., bong, Mr., bong, Mr., bong.

TWENTIETH-CENTURY BLUES

What do you call it, bobsled champion, and you, too, Olympic
    roller-coaster ace,
High-diving queen, what is the word,
Number one man on the Saturday poker squad, motion-picture
    star incognito as a home girl, life of the party or you, the
    serious type, what is it, what is it,

When it's just like a fever shooting up and up and up but there
    are no chills and there is no fever,
Just exactly like a song, like a knockout, like a dream, like a book,

What is the word, when you know that all the lights of all the
    cities of all the world are burning bright as day, and you
    know that some time they all go out for you,
Or your taxi rolls and rolls through streets made of velvet, what
    is the feeling, what is the feeling when the radio never
    ends, but the hour, the swift, the electric, the invisible hour
    does not stop and does not turn,
What does it mean, when the get-away money burns in dollars big
    as moons, but where is there to go that's just exactly right,
What have you won, plunger, when the 20-to-1 comes in; what
    have you won, salesman, when the dotted line is signed;
    irresistible lover, when her eyelids flutter shut at last, what
    have you really, finally won;
And what is gone, soldier, soldier, step-and-a-half marine who saw
    the whole world; hot-tip addict, what is always just missed;.
    picker of crumbs, how much has been lost, denied, what
    are all the things destroyed,
Question mark, question mark, question mark, question mark,
And you, fantasy Frank, and dreamworld Dora and hallucination
    Harold, and delusion Dick, and nightmare Ned,

What is it, how do you say it, what does it mean, what's the word,
That miracle thing, the thing that can't be so, quote, unquote, but
      just the same it's true,
That third-rail, million-volt exclamation mark, that ditto, ditto,
      ditto,
That stop, stop, go.

DENOUEMENT

1

Sky, be blue, and more than blue; wind, be flesh and blood; flesh
    and blood, be deathless;
Walls, streets, be home;
Desire of millions, become more real than warmth and breath and
    strength and bread;
Clock, point to the decisive hour and, hour without name when
    stacked and waiting murder fades, dissolves, stay forever as
    the world grows new—

Truth, be known, be kept forever, let the letters, letters, souvenirs,
    documents, snapshots, bills be found at last, be torn away
    from a world of lies, be kept as final evidence, transformed
    forever into more than truth;
Change, change, rows and rows and rows of figures, spindles,
    furrows, desks, change into paid-up rent and let the paid-up
    rent become South Sea music;
Magic film, unwind, unroll, unfold in silver on that million mile
    screen, take us all, bear us again to the perfect denoue-
    ment—

Where everything lost, needed, each forgotten thing, all that
    never happens,
Gathers at last into a dynamite triumph, a rainbow peace, a thun-
    derbolt kiss,
For you, the invincible, and I, grown older, and he, the shipping
    clerk, and she, an underweight blonde journeying home in
    the last express.

2

But here is the body found lying face down in a burlap sack,
    strangled in the noose jerked shut by these trussed and
    twisted and frantic arms;
But here are the agents, come to seize the bed;

But here is the vase holding saved-up cigar-store coupons, and
    here is a way to save on cigars and to go without meat;
But here is the voice that strikes around the world, "My friends
    . . . my friends," issues from the radio and thunders "My
    friends" in newsreel close-ups, explodes across headlines,
    "Both rich and poor, my friends, must sacrifice," re-echoes,
    murmuring, through hospitals, death-cells, "My friends
    . . . my friends . . . my friends . . . my friends . . ."

And who, my friend, are you?
Are you the one who leaped to the blinds of the cannon-ball ex-
    press? Or are you the one who started life again with three
    dependents and a pack of cigarettes?—

But how can these things be made finally clear in a post-mortem
    scene with the lips taped shut and the blue eyes cold, wide,
    still, blind, fixed beyond the steady glare of electric lights,
    through the white-washed ceiling and the cross-mounted
    roof, past the drifting clouds?—

Objection, over-ruled, exception, proceed:—

Was yours the voice heard singing one night in a fly-blown, soot-
    beamed, lost and forgotten Santa Fe saloon? Later bellow-
    ing in rage? And you boiled up a shirt in a Newark
    furnished room? Then you found another job, and pledged
    not to organize, or go on strike?—

We offer this union book in evidence. We offer these rent receipts
    in evidence. We offer this vacation card marked, "This is
    the life. Regards to all."—

You, lodge member, protestant, crossborn male, the placenta dis-
    colored, at birth, by syphilis, you, embryo four inches deep
    in the seventh month,
Among so many, many sparks struck and darkened at conception,
Which were you,
You, six feet tall on the day of death?—

Then you were at no time the senator's son? Then you were never
    the beef king's daughter, married in a storm of perfume and
    music and laughter and rice?
And you are not now the clubman who waves and nods and
    vanishes to Rio in a special plane?
But these are your lungs, scarred and consumed? These are your
    bones, still marked by rickets? These are your pliers? These
    are your fingers, O master mechanic, and these are your
    cold, wide, still, blind eyes?—

The witness is lying, lying, an enemy, my friends, of Union Gas
    and the home:—

But how will you know us, wheeled from the icebox and stretched
    upon the table with the belly slit wide and the entrails
    removed, voiceless as the clippers bite through ligaments
    and flesh and nerves and bones,
How will you know us, attentive, strained, before the director's
    desk, or crowded in line in front of factory gates,
How will you know us through ringed machinegun sights as we
    run and fall in gasmask, helmet, flame-tunic, uniform,
    bayonet, pack,
How will you know us, crumbled into ashes, lost in air and water
    and fire and stone,
How will you know us, now or any time, who will ever know that
    we have lived or died?—

And this is the truth? So help you God, this is the truth? The truth
    in full, so help you God? So help you God?
But the pride that was made of iron and could not be broken,
    what has become of it, what has become of the faith that
    nothing could destroy, what has become of the deathless
    hope,

You, whose ways were yours alone, you, the one like no one else,
what have you done with the hour you swore to remember,
where is the hour, the day, the achievement that would
never die?—

Morphine. Veronal. Veronal. Morphine. Morphine. Morphine.
Morphine.

3
Leaflets, scraps, dust, match-stubs strew the linoleum that leads
upstairs to the union hall, the walls of the basement work-
ers' club are dim and cracked and above the speaker's
stand Vanzetti's face shows green, behind closed doors the
committeeroom is a fog of smoke—

Who are these people?—

All day the committee fought like cats and dogs and twelve of
Mr. Kelly's strongarm men patrolled the aisles that night,
them blackjack guys get ten to twenty bucks a throw, the
funds were looted, sent to Chicago, at the meeting the
organizer talked like a fool, more scabs came through in
trucks guarded by police,
Workers of the world, workers of the world, workers of the
world—

Who are these people and what do they want, can't they be de-
cent, can't they at least be calm and polite,
Besides the time is not yet ripe, it might take years, like Mr. Kelly
said, years—

Decades black with famine and red with war, centuries on fire,
ripped wide—

Who are these people and what do they want, why do they walk
back and forth with signs that say "Bread Not Bullets,"
what do they mean "They Shall Not Die" as they sink in
clouds of poison gas and fall beneath clubs, hooves, rifles,
fall and do not arise, arise, unite,
Never again these faces, arms, eyes, lips—

Not unless we live, and live again,
Return, everywhere alive in the issue that returns, clear as light
that still descends from a star long cold, again alive and
everywhere visible through and through the scene that
comes again, as light on moving water breaks and returns,
heard only in the words, as millions of voices become one
voice, seen only in millions of hands that move as one—

Look at them gathered, raised, look at their faces, clothes, who
are these people, who are these people,
What hand scrawled large in the empty prison cell "I have just
received my sentence of death: Red Front," whose voice
screamed out in the silence "Arise"?—

And all along the waterfront, there, where rats gnaw into the
loading platforms, here, where the wind whips at ware-
house corners, look, there, here,
Everywhere huge across the walls and gates "Your comrades live,"
Where there is no life, no breath, no sound, no touch, no warmth,
no light but the lamp that shines on a trooper's drawn and
ready bayonet.

No violence,
Feeling may run high for a time, but remember, no violence,
And hurry, this moment of ours may not return.

But we will meet again? Yes, yes, now go,
Take only the latest instruments, use trained men in conservative
    tweeds who know how to keep their mouths shut,
The key positions must he held at all costs,
Bring guns, ropes, kerosene, it may be hard to persuade our be-
    loved leader there must be no violence, no violence,

No violence, nothing left to chance, no hysteria and above all,
    no sentiment,
The least delay, the slightest mistake means the end, yes, the end—
Why, are you worried?

What is there to be worried about? It's fixed, I tell you, fixed,
    there's nothing to it, listen:
We will meet across the continents and years at 4 A.M. outside
    the Greek's when next the barometer reads 28.28 and the
    wind is from the South South-East bringing rain and hail
    and fog and snow;
Until then I travel by dead reckoning and you will take your
    bearings from the stars;

I cannot tell you more, except this: When you give the sign our
    agent will approach and say, "Have you seen the hand-
    writing?" Then your man is to reply, "We have brought
    the money";
So we will make ourselves known to each other,
And it will be the same as before, perhaps even better, and we
    will arrange to meet again, as always, and say good-bye as
    now, and as we always will, and it will be O.K.; now go—

But what if the police find out? What if the wires are down? What
    if credit is refused? What if the banks fail? What if war
    breaks out? What if one of us should die?
What good can all of this be to you, or to us, or to anyone? Think
    of the price—

What are you trying to do, be funny? This is serious;
Hurry;
We must be prepared for anything, anything, anything.

MEMO

Is there still any shadow there, on the rainwet window of the
    coffee pot,
Between the haberdasher's and the pinball arcade,
There, where we stood one night in the warm, fine rain, and
    smoked and laughed and talked.

Is there now any sound at all,
Other than the sound of tires, and motors, and hurrying feet,
Is there on tonight's damp, heelpocked pavement somewhere the
    mark of a certain toe, an especial nail, or the butt of a
    particular dropped cigarette?—

(There must be, there has to be, no heart could beat if this were
    not so,
That was an hour, a glittering hour, an important hour in a tre-
    mendous year)

Where we talked for a while of life and love, of logic and the
    senses, of you and of me, character and fate, pain, revo-
    lution, victory and death,

Is there tonight any shadow, at all,
Other than the shadows that stop for a moment and then hurry
    past the windows blurred by the same warm, slow, still
    rain?

A DOLLAR'S WORTH OF BLOOD, PLEASE

With the last memo checked: *They will sign, success;* with the
  phone put down upon the day's last call; then with the
  door locked at last,
Wait; think;
What should the final memo be?

SAY THE LAST WORD,
SAY THE LAST WORD ADDING ALL WE'VE MADE AND LOST,
SAY THE LAST WORD THAT WEIGHS THE TRIUMPH SEALED IN INK
  AGAINST THE DEBT PRESERVED IN STONE AND THE PROFIT
  LOCKED IN STEEL,

One final word that the doorman knows, too, and the lawyer, and
  the drunk,
That the clerk knows, too, sure of tomorrow's pleasant surprise,
And the stranger, who knows there is nothing on earth more
  costly than hope and nothing in all the world held one-half
  so cheap as life,

One final word that need never be changed,
One final word to prove there is a use for the hard-bought distrust
  and the hard-won skill,
One final word that stands above and beyond the never-ending
  weakness and the never-failing strength,

SAY THE LAST WORD, YOU LONG STRAIGHT STREETS,
SAY THE LAST WORD, YOU WISE GUY, DUMB GUY, SOFT GUY, RIGHT
  GUY, FALL GUY, TOUGH GUY,
SAY THE LAST WORD, YOU BLACK SKY ABOVE.

LITERARY

I sing of simple people and the hardier virtues, by Associated
   Stuffed Shirts & Company, Incorporated, 358 West 42d
   Street, New York, brochure enclosed;
Of Christ on the Cross, by a visitor to Calvary, first class;
Art deals with eternal, not current verities, revised from last
   week's Sunday supplement;
Guess what we mean, in *The Literary System;* and a thousand
   noble answers to a thousand empty questions, by a patriot
   who needs the dough.

And so it goes.
Books are the key to magic portals. Knowledge is power. Give
   the people light.
Writing must be such a nice profession.
Fill in the coupon. How do you know? Maybe you can be a
   writer, too.

HAPPY NEW YEAR

Speak as you used to;
Make the drinks and talk while you mix them, as you have so
  many times before;

IF IT IS TRUE THAT THE WORLD IS FOR SALE

Then say it, say it once and forget it, drop it, tell how it was at
  bridge or the grocer's,
Repeat what you said, what the grocer said, what the errand boy
  said, what the janitor said,
Say anything at all,

BUT IF IT IS TRUE THAT THE NERVE AND BREATH AND PULSE ARE
  FOR SALE

Tell how it was in some gayer city or brighter place, speak of
  some bloodier, hungrier, more treacherous land,
Any other age, any far land,

BUT IF IT IS TRUE

Forget the answers that give no reason, forget the reasons that
  do not explain;
Do you remember the day at the lake, the evening at Sam's, the
  petrified forest, would you like to see London in June
  once more?

BUT IF IT IS TRUE, IF IT IS TRUE THAT ONLY LIARS LOVE TRUTH

Pour the cocktails,
It is late, it is cold, it is still, it is dark;
Quickly, for time is swift and it is late, late, later than you think,
With one more hour, one more night, one more day somehow to
  be killed.

DEVIL'S DREAM

But it could never be true;
How could it ever happen, if it never did before, and it's not so
     now?

But suppose that the face behind those steel prison bars—
Why do you dream about a face lying cold in the trenches streaked
     with rain and dirt and blood?
Is it the very same face seen so often in the mirror?
Just as though it could be true—

But what if it is, what if it is, what if it is, what if the thing that
     cannot happen really happens just the same,
Suppose the fever goes a hundred, then a hundred and one,
What if Holy Savings Trust goes from 98 to 88 to 78 to 68, then
     drops down to 28 and 8 and out of sight,
And the fever shoots a hundred two, a hundred three, a hundred
     four, then a hundred five and out?

But now there's only the wind and the sky and sunlight and the
     clouds,
With everyday people walking and talking as they always have
     before along the everyday street,
Doing ordinary things with ordinary faces and ordinary voices in
     the ordinary way,
Just as they always will—

Then why does it feel like a bomb, why does it feel like a target,
Like standing on the gallows with the trap about to drop,
Why does it feel like a thunderbolt the second before it strikes,
     why does it feel like a tight-rope walk high over hell?

Because it is not, will not, never could be true
That the whole wide, bright, green, warm, calm world goes:
CRASH.

42

HOLD THE WIRE

If the doorbell rings, and we think we were followed here; or if
      the bell should ring but we are not sure—
How can we decide?

IF IT'S ONLY THE GAS-MAN it may be all right,
IF HE'S AN AUTHORIZED PERSON IN A DOUBLE-BREASTED SUIT we'd
      better get it over with,
IF HE'S SOME NOBODY it may be good news,
But it might mean death IF THE SAMPLES ARE FREE,

HOW DO WE KNOW YOU'RE THE PERSON THAT YOU SAY?

Decide, decide,
We'd better be certain, if we live just once, and the sooner the
      better if we must decide,

BUT NOT IF IT'S WAR,
Not until we've counted the squares on the wallpaper over again,
      and added up the circles, and the circles match the
      squares—
Shall we move to the Ritz if rails go up, or live in potter's field if
      the market goes down?
If they sign for peace we return to the city, if they burn and bomb
      the city we will go to the mountains—
Who will kill us, if they do, and who will carry on our work?

Who are you, who are you, you have the right number but the
      connection's very poor;
We can hear you well enough, but we don't like what you're
      saying;
Yes, the order was received, but we asked for something else—

Are you the inventor who wants to sell us an invisible man?
WE'D CERTAINLY LIKE TO BUY HIM BUT WE HAVEN'T GOT THE PRICE;

Are you someone very famous from the Missing Persons Bureau
  but you can't recall the name?
COME AROUND NEXT AUGUST, WE'RE BUSY AS HELL TODAY;
If it's another bill collector there is no one here at all;

If it's Adolf Hitler, if it's the subway gorilla, if it's Jack the Ripper,
SEND HIM IN, SEND HIM IN, IF IT'S JOLLY JACK THE RIPPER IN A
  DOUBLE-BREASTED SUIT AND THE SAMPLES ARE FREE.

HOW DO I FEEL?

Get this straight, Joe, and don't get me wrong.
Sure, Steve, O.K., all I got to say is, when do I get the dough?

Will you listen for a minute? And just shut up? Let a guy explain?
Go ahead, Steve, I won't say a word.

Will you just shut up?
O.K., I tell you, whatever you say, it's O.K. with me.

What's O.K. about it, if that's the way you feel?
What do you mean, how I feel? What do you know, how I feel?

Listen, Joe, a child could understand, if you'll listen for a minute
    without butting in, and don't get so sore.
Sure, I know, you got to collect it first before you lay it out, I
    know that; you can't be left on a limb yourself.

Me? On a limb? For a lousy fifty bucks?
Take it easy, Steve, I'm just saying—

I'm just telling you—
Wait, listen—

Now listen, wait, will you listen for a minute? That's all I ask.
    Yes or no?
O.K., I only—

Yes or no?
O.K., O.K.

O.K., then, and you won't get sore? If I tell it to you straight?
Sure, Steve, O.K., all I got to say is, when do I get the dough?

Q & A

Where analgesia may be found to ease the infinite, minute scars
    of the day;
What final interlude will result, picked bit by bit from the morn-
    ing's hurry, the lunch-hour boredom, the fevers of the
    night;
Why this one is cherished by the gods, and that one not;
How to win, and win again, and again, staking wit alone against
    a sea of time;
Which man to trust and, once found, how far—

Will not be found in Matthew, Mark, Luke, or John,
Nor Blackstone, nor Gray's, nor Dun & Bradstreet, nor Freud,
    nor Marx,
Nor the sage of the evening news, nor the corner astrologist, nor
    in any poet,

Nor what sort of laughter should greet the paid pronouncements
    of the great,
Nor what pleasure the multitudes have, bringing lunch and the
    children to watch the condemned be plunged into death,

Nor why the sun should rise tomorrow,
Nor how the moon still weaves upon the ground, through the
    leaves, so much silence and so much peace.

PANTOMIME

She sleeps, lips round, see how at rest,
How dark the hair, unstrung with all the world;
See the desirable eyes, how still, how white, sealed to all faces,
     locked against ruin, favor, and every risk,

Nothing behind them now but a pale mirage,
Through which the night-time ragman of the street below moves
     in a stiff and slow ballet,
Rhythmic from door to door, hallway to curb and gutter to stoop,
     bat's eyes bright, ravenous, ravenous for the carrion found
     and brought by tireless fingers to unreal lips;

Her hand relaxed beside the enchanted head, mouth red, small,
See how at peace the human form can be, whose sister, whose
     sweetheart, daughter of whom, and now the adorable ears,
     coral and pink,
Deaf to every footfall, every voice,
Midnight threats, the rancor stifled in rented bedrooms, appeals
     urged across kitchen tables and the fury that shouts them
     down, gunfire, screams, the sound of pursuit,
All of these less than the thunderous wings of a moth that circles
     here in the room where she sleeps,

Sleeps, dreaming that she sleeps and dreams.

LONGSHOT BLUES

What if all the money is bet on the odd;
Maybe the even wins,
What if odd wins, but it wins too late,

Whoever, wherever,
Ever knows who will be just the very one
This identical day at just this very, very, very, very hour,

Whose whole life falls between roto-press wheels moving quicker
    than light, to reappear, gorgeous and calm, on page eight-
    een,
Who reads all about it: *Prize-winning beauty trapped, accused,*

Who rides, and rides, and rides the big bright limited south, or is
    found, instead, on the bedroom floor with a stranger's bullet
    through the middle of his heart,
Clutching at a railroad table of trains to the south while the cur-
    tains blow wild and the radio plays and the sun shines on,
    and on, and on, and on,
Never having dreamed, at 9 o'clock, it would ever, at 10 o'clock,
    end this way,

Forever feeling certain, but never quite guessing just exactly
    right,
As no man, anywhere, ever, ever, ever, ever, ever knows for sure—

Who wins the limousine, who wins the shaving cup, who nearly
    wins the million-dollar sweeps,
Who sails, and sails, and sails the seven seas,
Who returns safe from the fight at the mill gates, or wins, and
    wins, and wins, and wins the plain pine coffin and a union
    cortege to a joblot grave?—

With that long black midnight hour at last exploding into rockets
    of gold,

With every single cloud in the sky forever white and every white
    cloud always the winner in its race with death,
With every pair of eyes burning brighter than the diamonds that
    burn on every throat,
With every single inch of the morning all yours and every single
    inch of the evening yours alone, and all of it always, al-
    ways, altogether new.

SOS

It is posted in the clubrooms,
It is announced in bright electric lights on all the principal streets,
      it is rumored, proclaimed, and radio'd out to sea,
SOS, SOS,
That her hair is a dark cloud and her eyes are deep blue;

Total strangers on the buses, at the beaches, in the parks,
Argue and discuss, as though they really knew,
Whether she prefers cork tips, likes a sweet or dry sherry, takes
      lemon with her tea,
SOS, SOS,

But they all agree that her hats, that her gowns, that her slippers,
      that her gloves, that her books, that her flowers,
And her past, and her present, and her future as stated in the
      cards, and as written in the stars,

Are all about right,
All dead right and dead against the law,

But her eyes are blue,
Blue for miles and miles and miles,
SOS, SOS,
Blue across the country and away across the sea.

A PATTERN

The alarm that shatters sleep, at least, is real;
Certainly the razor is real, and there is no denying the need for
      coffee and an egg;
Are there any questions, or is this quite clear, and true?

Surely it is morning, and in the mail the chainstore people offer
      a new Fall line;
There is a bill for union dues, a request for additional support;
Then the news: somewhere a million men are on the march again,
      elsewhere the horror mounts; and there are incidental lep-
      rosies—
(Briefly, here, the recollection of some old, imagined splendor,
      to be quickly dropped and crushed completely out.)

Are there any questions?
Has anyone any objections to make?
Can a new political approach or a better private code evolve from
      this?
Does it hold any premise based on faith alone?

Or are you, in fact, a privileged ghost returned, as usual, to haunt
      yourself?
A vigorous, smiling corpse come back to tour the morgues?
To inspect the scene of the silent torture and the invisible death,
      and then to report?

And if to report, are there any different answers now, at last?

Tomorrow, yes, tomorrow,
There will suddenly be new success, like Easter clothes, and a
strange and different fate,
And bona-fide life will arrive at last, stepping from a non-stop
monoplane with chromium doors and a silver wing and
straight white staring lights.

There will be the sound of silvery thunder again to stifle the in-
sane silence;
A new, tremendous sound will shatter the final unspoken ques-
tion and drown the last, mute, terrible reply;
Rockets, rockets, Roman candles, flares, will burst in every corner
of the night, to veil with snakes of silvery fire the nothing-
ness that waits and waits;
There will be a bright, shimmering, silver veil stretched every-
where, tight, to hide the deep, black, empty, terrible bot-
tom of the world where people fall who are alone, or dead,

Sick or alone,
Alone or poor,
Weak, or mad, or doomed, or alone;

Tomorrow, yes, tomorrow, surely we begin at last to live,
With lots and lots of laughter,
Solid silver laughter,
Laughter, with a few simple instructions, and a bona-fide guar-
antee.

PORTRAIT

The clear brown eyes, kindly and alert, with 12-20 vision, give
     confident regard to the passing world through R. K. Lam-
     pert & Company lenses framed in gold;
His soul, however, is all his own;
Arndt Brothers necktie and hat (with feather) supply a touch of
     youth.

With his soul his own, he drives, drives, chats and drives,
The first and second bicuspids, lower right, replaced by bridge-
     work, while two incisors have porcelain crowns;

(Render unto Federal, state, and city Caesar, but not unto time;
Render nothing unto time until Amalgamated Death serves final
     notice, in proper form;

The vault is ready;
The will has been drawn by Clagget, Clagget, Clagget & Brown;
The policies are adequate, Confidential's best, reimbursing for dis-
     ability, partial or complete, with double indemnity should
     the end be a pure and simple accident)

Nothing unto time,
Nothing unto change, nothing unto fate,
Nothing unto you, and nothing unto me, or to any other known or
     unknown party or parties, living or deceased;

But Mercury shoes, with special arch supports, take much of the
     wear and tear;
On the course, a custombuilt driver corrects a tendency to slice;
Love's ravages have been repaired (it was a textbook case) by
     Drs. Schultz, Lightner, Mannheim, and Goode,
While all of it is enclosed in excellent tweed, with Mr. Baumer's
     personal attention to the shoulders and the waist;

And all of it now roving, chatting amiably through space in a
    Plymouth 6,
With his soul (his own) at peace, soothed by Walter Lippmann,
    and sustained by Haig & Haig.

DEBRIS

The windows, faintly blue and gold in the sun's first light;
The mirages of the night suddenly replaced by the familiar room;
There is the empty bottle again, and the shattered glass (do you
      remember?);
Once more the light left burning in the lamp, and again the clut-
      tered table-top (do you remember that?).

Do the faces and the words come back to you;
Do all the things the drinking and the talk once more blotted out
      come back to you now,
With bitter cigarettes in the morning air?

It strikes and strikes, insane but true: This life, this life, this life,
      this life;
While mist rises from the cool valleys,
And somewhere in fresh green hills there is the singing of a bird.

TOMORROW

Now that the others are gone, all of them, forever,
And they have your answer, and you have theirs, and the decision
     is made,
And the river of minutes between you widens to a tide of hours, a
     flood of days, a gulf of years and a sea of silence;

If, now, there are any questions you would like to ask of the shapes
     that still move and speak inaudibly in the empty room,
If there are any different arrangements you would like to suggest,

Make them to the riverboats, whose echoing whistle will be a
     clear reply,
Speak to the seagulls, their effortless flight will provide any an-
     swer you may wish to hear,
Ask the corner chestnut vendor, ask the tireless hammer and pulse
     of the subway,
Speak to the family on the illuminated billboard, forever friendly,
     or to the wind, or to the sign that sways and creaks above
     the stationer's door.

REQUIEM

Will they stop,
Will they stand there for a moment, perhaps before some shop
     where you have gone so many times
(Stand with the same blue sky above them and the stones, so often
     walked, beneath)

Will it be a day like this—
As though there could be such a day again—

And will their own concerns still be about the same,
And will the feeling still be this that you have felt so many times,
Will they meet and stop and speak, one perplexed and one aloof,

Saying: Have you heard,
Have you heard,
Have you heard about the death?

Yes, choosing the words, tragic, yes, a shock,
One who had so much of this, they will say, a life so filled with
     that,
Then will one say that the days are growing crisp again, the other
     that the leaves are turning,
And will they say good-bye, good-bye, you must look me up some
     time, good-bye,
Then turn and go, each of them thinking, and yet, and yet,

Each feeling, if it were I, instead, would that be all,
Each wondering, suddenly alone, if that is all, in fact—

And will that be all?
On a day like this, with motors streaming through the fresh parks,
     the streets alive with casual people,
And everywhere, on all of it, the brightness of the sun.

C STANDS FOR CIVILIZATION

They are able, with science, to measure the millionth of a mil-
lionth of an electron-volt,
THE TWENTIETH CENTURY COMES BUT ONCE
The natives can take to caves in the hills, said the British M.P.,
when we bomb their huts,
THE TWENTIETH CENTURY COMES BUT ONCE

Electric razors;
I am the law, said Mayor Hague;
The lynching was televised, we saw the whole thing from begin-
ning to end, we heard the screams and the crackle of flames
in a soundproof room,
THE TWENTIETH CENTURY COMES BUT ONCE

You are born but once,
You have your chance to live but once,
You go mad and put a bullet through your head but once,

THE TWENTIETH CENTURY COMES BUT ONCE
Once too soon, or a little too late, just once too often,

But zooming through the night in Lockheed monoplanes the
witches bring accurate pictures of the latest disaster ex-
actly on time,
THE TWENTIETH CENTURY COMES BUT ONCE
ONLY ONCE, AND STAYS FOR BUT ONE HUNDRED YEARS.

LUNCH WITH THE SOLE SURVIVOR

Meaning what it seems to when the day's receipts are counted
  and locked inside the store and the keys are taken home;
Feeling as it does to drive a car that rides and rides like a long,
  low, dark, silent streak of radio waves;
Just the way the hero feels in a smash-hit show;
Exactly like the giant in a Times Square sign making love across
  the sky to a lady made of light;

And then as though the switch were thrown and all of the lights
  went out;
Then as though the curtain fell and then they swept the aisles
  and then it's someone's turn to go,
Smoke the last cigarette, drink the last tall drink, go with the last
  long whistle of the midnight train as it fades among the
  hills—

Meaning what it seems to mean but feeling the way it does,
As though the wind would always, always blow away from home.

TAKE A LETTER

Would you like to live, yourself, the way that other people do,
Would you like to be the kind of man you've always dreamed
    you'd be,
Do you know that tax consultants get very good pay,
Or would you rather become a detective, and trap your man,

ARREST HIM, ARREST HIM
How do you know you can't compose
ARREST THAT MAN
Would you like to have poise, speak Russian, Spanish, French,

ARREST THAT MAN, HE FITS THE DESCRIPTION PERFECTLY
Maybe you, too, can paint,
I KNOW HIM FROM HIS PICTURE, IT WAS IN THE MORNING PAPERS
Want to stop the tobacco habit, like to study aviation, own a
    genuine diamond ring,

I TELL YOU, IT'S HIM
Do you crawl with crazy urges,
Get those wild, wild feelings that you can't control,
IT'S HIM, IT'S HIM, HE'S HERE AGAIN, HE'S WANTED, IT'S HIM

Feel a big, strange, jumpy, weird, crazy new impulse,
Want to own your own home and wear the very best clothes,
Would you like to live and love and learn as other people do,

STOP HIM, HE SOUNDS JUST EXACTLY LIKE THE MISSING BOSTON HEIR
HOLD HIM, HE MIGHT EVEN BE THE SENATOR FROM THE SOUTH
    WHOSE MIND WENT BLANKER STILL
ARREST THAT MAN, HE FITS THE HUMAN GIRAFFE FROM A TO Z

But he never could be you,
The most impressive bankrupt in the most exclusive club,
Or the mildest, coolest madman on the whole Eastern coast.

RADIO BLUES

Try 5 on the dial, try 10, 15;
Just the ghost of an inch, did you know, divides Japan and Peru?
20, 25;
Is that what you want, static and a speech and the fragment of a
      waltz, is that just right?
Or what do you want at twelve o'clock, with the visitors gone, and
      the Scotch running low?

30, 35, 35 to 40 and 40 to 50;
Free samples of cocoa, and the Better Beer Trio, and hurricane
      effects for a shipwreck at sea,
But is that just right to match the feeling that you have?

From 60 to 70 the voice in your home may be a friend of yours,
From 70 to 80 the voice in your home may have a purpose of its
      own,
From 80 to 90 the voice in your home may bring you love, or war,
But is that what you want?

100, 200, 300, 400;
Would you like to tune in on the year before last?
500, 600,
Or the decade after this, with the final results of the final madness
      and the final killing?

600, 700, 800, 900;
What program do you want at midnight, or at noon, at three in
      the morning,
At 6 A.M. or at 6 P.M.,
With the wind still rattling the windows, and shaking the blinds?

Would you care to bring in the stations past the stars?
Would you care to tune in on your dead love's grave?

1000, 2000, 3000, 4000;
Is that just right to match the feeling that you want?
5000, 6000;
Is that just right?
7000, 8000;
Is that what you want to match the feeling that you have?
9000, 10,000;
Would you like to tune in upon your very own life, gone some-
    where far away?

Why do you glance above you, for a moment, before you stop
    and go inside,
Why do you lay aside the book in the middle of the chapter to
    rise and walk to the window and stare into the street,
What do you listen for, briefly, among the afternoon voices, that
    the others do not,
Where are your thoughts, when the train whistles or the tele-
    phone rings, that you turn your head,
Why do you look, so often, at the calendar, the clock?

What rainbow waits, especially, for you,
Who will call your number, that angel chorales will float across
    the wire,
What magic score do you hope to make,
What final sweeps do you expect to win that the sky will drop
    clusters of stars in your hair and rain them at your feet,
What do you care whose voice, whose face, what hour, what
    day, what month, what year?

MANHATTAN

Deep city,

Tall city, worn city, switchboard weaving what ghost horizons
(who commands this cable, who escapes from this net, who
shudders in this web?), cold furnace in the sky,

Guardian of this man's youth, graveyard of the other's, jailer of
mine,

Harassed city, city knowing and naive, gay in the theaters, wary
in the offices, starved in the tenements,

City ageless in the hospital delivery rooms and always too old or
too young in the echoing morgues—

City for sale, for rent:

Five rooms, the former tenant's mattress, still warm, is leaving on
the van downstairs;

Move in;

Here are the keys to the mailbox, the apartment, and the outside
door,

It is yours, all yours, this city, this street, this house designed by
a famous architect, you would know the name at once,

This house where the suicide lived, perhaps this floor, this room
that reflects the drugstore's neon light;

Here, where the Wall Street clerk, the engineer, the socialist, the
music teacher all lived by turns,

Move in,

Move in, arrange the furniture and live, live, go in the morning
to return at night,

Relax, plan, struggle, succeed, watch the snow fall and hear the
rain beat, know the liner's voice, see the evening plane, a
star among stars, go west at the scheduled hour,

Make so many phone calls in the foyer again, have so many busi-
ness talks in the livingroom, there will be cocktails, cards,
and the radio, adultery again (downtown), vomit (again)
in the bath,

Scenes, hysterics, peace,

Live, live, live, and then move out,

64

Go with the worn cabinets and rugs all piled on the curb while
the city passes and the incoming tenant (unknown to you)
awaits,
Yes, go,
But remember, remember that, that year, that season—

Do you, do you, do you,
City within city, sealed fortress within fortress, island within en-
chanted island,
Do you, there outside the stationer's shop, still hear gunfire and
instant death on winter nights,
Still see, on bright Spring afternoons, a thin gray figure crumple
to the walk in the park
(Who stared, who shrugged and went home, who stayed and
shivered until the ambulance arrived?—
Let the spirit go free, ship the body west),
Do you remember that, do you,
Do you remember the missing judge, the bigshot spender and the
hundred dollar bills (did he do three years?),
The ballgame of ballgames (the fourth in the series, or was that
the sixth?),
The reform party and the gambling clean-up (a ten-day laugh),
the returning champion (what about it?), the abortion
(so what?), the rape (who cares?),
The paralyzed newsboy, the taxi-driver who studied dramatics,
the honest counterman, the salesman in love with the
aviator's wife, the day at the zoo, the evening in the park,
the perfect girl, the funny little guy with the funny little
face—

City, city, city,
Eye without vision, light without warmth, voice without mind,
pulse without flesh,
Mirror and gateway, mirage, cloud against the sun,

Do you remember that, that year, that day, that hour, that name,
that face,
Do you remember:

Only the day, fulfilled, as it burns in the million windows of the
west,
Only the promise of the day, returning, as it flames on the roofs
and spires and steeples of the east.

SCHEHERAZADE

Not the saga of your soul at grips with fate, bleedingheart, for
we have troubles of our own,
Nor the inside story of the campaign scandal, wise-guy, for we
were there ourselves, or else we have forgotten it years ago;
Not all the answers, oracle, to politics and life and love; you have
them, but your book is out of date;
No, nor why you are not a heel, smooth baby, for that is a lie, nor
why you had to become one, for that is much too true,
Nor the neighborhood doings five years ago, rosebud, nor the
ruined childhood, nor the total story of friendship betrayed,
Nor how cynical you are, rumpot, and why you became so;

Give us, instead (if you must), something that we can use, like
a telephone number,
Or something we can understand, like a longshot tip on tomor-
row's card,
Or something that we have never heard before, like the legend
of Ruth.

The subject was put to bed at midnight, and I picked him up
again at 8 A.M.

I followed, as usual, while he made his morning rounds.

After him, and like him, I stepped into taxis, pressed elevator
buttons, fed tokens into subway turnstiles, kept him under
close surveillance while he dodged through heavy traffic
and pushed through revolving doors.

We lunched very pleasantly, though separately, for $1.50, plus
a quarter tip. (Unavoidable expense.)

Then we resumed. For twenty minutes on the corner the subject
watched two shoeshine boys fish for a dime dropped
through a subway grate. No dice.

And then on. We had a good stare into a window made of invisible
glass.

Another hour in a newsreel movie—the usual famine, fashions,
Florida bathing, and butchery. Then out again.

I realized, presently, that the subject was following a blonde dish
in blue he had seen somewhere around.

(Nothing, ultimately, came of this.)

And shortly after that a small black pooch, obviously lost, at-
tached himself to your agent's heels.

Does he fit into this picture anywhere at all?

It doesn't matter. In any case, I resign.

Because the situation, awkward to begin with, swiftly developed
angles altogether too involved.

Our close-knit atomic world (night would disperse it) woven of
indifference (the blonde's), of love (the subject's), of sus-
picion (my province), and of forlorn hope (the dog's), this
little world became a social structure, and then a solar
system with dictates of its own.

We had our own world's fair in a pinball arcade. The blonde had
her picture taken in a photomat.

68

And so (whether by law, or by magnetism) did we.
But still there was nothing, in any of this, essentially new to report.

Except, I began to think of all the things the subject might have
    done, but he did not do.
All the exciting scenes he might have visited but failed to visit, all
    the money I might have watched him make or helped him
    spend, the murders he might have committed, but somehow
    he refrained.
What if he met a visiting star from the coast? And she had a
    friend?
Or went to Havana, or the South Sea Isles?
Did my instructions, with expenses, cover the case?
But none of this happened. Therefore, I resign.

I resign, because I do not think this fellow knew what he was
    doing.
I do not believe the subject knew, at all clearly, what he was
    looking for, or from what escaping.
Whether from a poor man's destiny (relief and the Bellevue
    morgue), or a middle-class fate (always the same job with
    a different firm), or from a Kreuger-Musica denouement.
And then, whose life am I really leading, mine or his? His or the
    blonde's?

And finally because this was his business, all of it, not mine.
Whatever conscience, boredom, or penal justice he sought to es-
    cape, it was his business, not mine in the least. I want no
    part of it.
I have no open or concealed passion for those doors we opened
    together, those turnstiles we pushed, those levers, handles,
    knobs.
Nor for the shadow of a bathing beauty on a screen, nor the pic-
    ture of a ruined village. Nor any interest in possible defects
    shown by invisible glass.

I mean, for instance, I do not (often) feel drawn toward that
particular type of blonde in that particular shade of blue.
And I have no room to keep a dog.

Therefore, this resignation.
Whether signed in a Turkish bath, with a quart of rye, or in a
good hotel, sealed with a bullet, is none of your business.
None at all.
There is no law compelling any man on earth to do the same,
second hand.
I am tired of following invisible lives down intangible avenues
to fathomless ends.
Is this clear?
Herewith, therefore, to take effect at once, I resign.

PACT

It is written in the skyline of the city (you have seen it, that bold
    and accurate inscription), where the gray and gold and
    soot-black roofs project against the rising or the setting sun,
It is written in the ranges of the farthest mountains, and written
    by the lightning bolt,
Written, too, in the winding rivers of the prairies, and in the
    strangely familiar effigies of the clouds,

That there will be other days and remoter times, by far, than
    these, still more prodigious people and still less credible
    events,
When there will be a haze, as there is today, not quite blue and
    not quite purple, upon the river, a green mist upon the
    valley below, as now,

And we will build, upon that day, another hope (because these
    cities are young and strong),
And we will raise another dream (because these hills and fields
    are rich and green),

And we will fight for all of this again, and if need be again,
And on that day, and in that place, we will try again, and this
    time we shall win.

This patient says he is troubled by insomnia, and that one finds it
difficult to stay awake.
Miss A confides a fear of narrow places. Mr. B, in Wall Street, is
everywhere pursued by a secret agent, and by a certain
X-ray eye that transmits his business secrets to a rival
clique.
Practice, in general, is good. The patients are of all classes. In
every case the problem is to exorcise these devils. And to
adjust.

To adjust the person to his gods, and to his own estate, and to the
larger group.
Adjust to the conventions and the niceties. That is, by inference, to
the Chamber of Commerce, to the local police, to the So-
ciety of Ancient Instruments, and to the West Side Bicycle
Club.
Adjust the kleptomaniac to modes of safer intercourse. The biga-
mist to the canons of the church, and to the criminal code.
(And all of these, perhaps, to him.)
Adjust the devils to the saints. The saints to the smiling devils.
The martyrs to the renegades, and each of them, alike, to
the hearty fools.

Adjust to the present, and to a longer view.
To cities shining in the sky tonight, and smoking in the dust
tomorrow.
Adjust the mothers. And the husbands. And the fathers. And the
wives.
Adjust to the sons, once resolute, now dead. And to the daughters,
living but mad.
Adjust to the morning crucifixion and the evening calm.
Adjust them all. And then adjust them to this new perspective.
Adjust.

Mr. X believes that tall brunettes can bring him only grief. Mrs. Y
    walks backward to escape the evil eye. Mr. Z hears voices.
They have nothing new to communicate, but he is disturbed.

Madness, never obsolete, grows fashionable.
Do its canons, unlike those of any other pursuit, seem to make
    unreasonable demands upon the patient?
Or require of the practitioner, himself, adjustments too fantastic,
    perhaps too terrible to reach?

HOMAGE

They said to him, "It is a very good thing that you have done,
yes, both good and great, proving this other passage to the
Indies. Marvelous," they said. "Very. But where, Señor, is
the gold?"

They said: "We like it, we admire it very much, don't misunder-
stand us, in fact we think it's almost great. But isn't there,
well, a little too much of this Prince of Denmark? After all,
there is no one quite like you in your lighter vein."

"Astonishing," they said. "Who would have thought you had it in
you, Orville?" They said, "Wilbur, this machine of yours
is amazing, if it works, and perhaps some day we can use
it to distribute eggs, or to advertise."

And they were good people, too. Decent people.

They did not beat their wives. They went to church. And they
kept the law.

Of you, both the known and unknown quantities, but more espe-
　　cially, of those unknown,
Of the mysteries of the arches and the ligaments, the question of
　　the nerves and muscles, the haunting riddle of the joints,
Of jetblack eyes and nutbrown hair,
Of the latest movie star, and Hollywood, and of a job that pays
　　real dough, and then of debts, current and past. The past?

Of the distant past. Of nutbrown eyes and jetblack hair. Of blue
　　eyes, and of yellow hair. Red hair and hazel eyes. Gray
　　eyes.
Of perfection: Can it ever be obtained?
Of time and change and chance. Right now, returning from Arc-
　　turus, of you.

Of the crazy hats and negligee in the shops along the avenue, of
　　perfume and of lace;
A startling fragment abruptly, here, shoots to the surface out of
　　early youth;
Of Freud, and of Krafft-Ebing for a moment. Of Havelock Ellis
　　(must read, some day, in full).

Is it like stepping into a looking-glass, or like flying through space?

Of the indubitable beginning of life, and of its indubitable end,
Of the mirage within a mirage,
With all of the daughters of all the daughters summed up, at last,
　　in you.

You have forgotten the monthly conference. Your four o'clock
appointment waits in the ante-room. The uptown bureau
is on the wire again.
Most of your correspondence is still unanswered, these bills have
not been paid, and one of your trusted agents has suddenly
resigned.
And where are this morning's reports? They must be filed at once,
at once.

It is an hour you do not fully understand, a mood you have had so
many times but cannot quite describe,
It is a fantastic situation repeated so often it is commonplace and
dull,
It is an unlikely plot, a scheme, a conspiracy you helped to begin
but do not, any longer, control at all.

Perhaps you are really in league with some maniac partner whom
you have never met, whose voice you have never heard,
whose name you do not even know.
It is a destiny that is yours, yours, all yours and only yours, a fate
you have long ago disowned and disavowed.

When they dig you up, in a thousand years, they will find you in
just this pose,
One hand upon the buzzer, the other reaching for the phone, eyes
fixed upon the calendar, feet firmly on the office rug.

Shall you ask the operator for an outside wire? And then dictate
this memo:
No (overwhelming) passions. No (remarkable) vices. No (memo-
rable) virtues. No (terrific) motives.

Yes, when they dig you up, like this, a thousand years from now,
They will say: Just as he was in life. A man typical of the times,
engaged in typical affairs.
Notice the features, especially, they will say. How self-assured
they are, and how serene.

ANY MAN'S ADVICE TO HIS SON

If you have lost the radio beam, then guide yourself by the sun or
the stars.
(By the North Star at night, and in daytime by the compass and
the sun.)
Should the sky be overcast and there are neither stars nor a sun,
then steer by dead reckoning.
If the wind and direction and speed are not known, then trust to
your wits and your luck.

Do you follow me? Do you understand? Or is this too difficult
to learn?
But you must and you will, it is important that you do,
Because there may be troubles even greater than these that I
have said.

Because, remember this: Trust no man fully.
Remember: If you must shoot at another man squeeze, do not
jerk the trigger. Otherwise you may miss and die, yourself,
at the hand of some other man's son.
And remember: In all this world there is nothing so easily squan-
dered, or once gone, so completely lost as life.

I tell you this because I remember you when you were small,
And because I remember all your monstrous infant boasts and lies,
And the way you smiled, and how you ran and climbed, as no one
else quite did, and how you fell and were bruised,
And because there is no other person, anywhere on earth, who
remembers these things as clearly as I do now.

A LA CARTE

Some take to liquor, some turn to prayer,
Many prefer to dance, others to gamble, and a few resort to gas
      or the gun.
(Some are lucky, and some are not.)

Name your choice, any selection from one to twenty-five:
Music from Harlem? A Viennese waltz on the slot-machine phono-
      graph at Jack's Bar & Grill? Or a Brahms Concerto over
      WXV?
(Many like it wild, others sweet.)

Champagne for supper, murder for breakfast, romance for lunch
      and terror for tea,
This is not the first time, nor will it be the last time the world has
      gone to hell.
(Some can take it, and some cannot.)

First you bite your fingernails. And then you comb your hair
again. And then you wait. And wait.
(They say, you know, that first you lie. And then you steal, they
say. And then, they say, you kill.)

Then the doorbell rings. Then Peg drops in. And Bill. And Jane.
And Doc.
And first you talk, and smoke, and hear the news and have a drink.
Then you walk down the stairs.
And you dine, then, and go to a show after that, perhaps, and
after that a night spot, and after that come home again,
and climb the stairs again, and again go to bed.

But first Peg argues, and Doc replies. First you dance the same
dance and you drink the same drink you always drank
before.
And the piano builds a roof of notes above the world.
And the trumpet weaves a dome of music through space. And the
drum makes a ceiling over space and time and night.
And then the table-wit. And then the check. Then home again to
bed.
But first, the stairs.

And do you now, baby, as you climb the stairs, do you still feel
as you felt back there?
Do you feel again as you felt this morning? And the night before?
And then the night before that?

(They say, you know, that first you hear voices. And then you have
visions, they say. Then, they say, you kick and scream and
rave.)
Or do you feel: What is one more night in a lifetime of nights?
What is one more death, or friendship, or divorce out of two, or
three? Or four? Or five?
One more face among so many, many faces, one more life among
so many million lives?

But first, baby, as you climb and count the stairs (and they total
   the same) did you, sometime or somewhere, have a differ-
   ent idea?
Is this, baby, what you were born to feel, and do, and be?

You recommend that the motive, in Chapter 8, should be changed
from ambition to a desire, on the heroine's part, for doing
good; yes, that can be done.

Installment 9 could be more optimistic, as you point out, and it
will not be hard to add a heartbreak to the class reunion in
Chapter 10.

Script 11 may have, as you say, too much political intrigue of the
sordid type; perhaps a diamond-in-the-rough approach
would take care of this. And 12 has a reference to war that,
as you suggest, had better be removed; yes.

This brings us to the holidays, that coincide with our prison se-
quence. With the convicts' Christmas supper, if you ap-
prove, we can go to town.

Yes, this should not be difficult. It can be done. Why not?

And script 600 brings us to the millennium, with all the fiends of
hell singing Bach chorales.

And in 601 we explore the Valleys of the Moon (why not?), find-
ing in each of them fresh Fountains of Youth.

And there is no mortal ill that cannot be cured by a little money,
or lots of love, or by a friendly smile; no.

And few human hopes go unrealized; no.

And the rain does not ever, anywhere, fall upon corroded monu-
ments and the graves of the forgotten dead.

Business of forcing a showdown.
Hit this hard, and take no excuses.
(Stuff about expenses. Business about the risks. Stuff about over-
head.)

If the bank should call, stall them off.
Don't say yes or no, but it has to sound good. Maybe gone for
the week.
Yes, left no word, but had hoped to be back, regret the delay and
so forth and so on, will definitely return on such-and-such
a date.

Lunch with so-and-so.
One highball, no more. Two at most. A walk to clear the head.

And stuff for all the other deals, for every possible turn and twist.
Wallop it hard. Keep them guessing. And naturally, no mistakes.
Cheerful stuff. Personality stuff. Courteous stuff.
Tough, if necessary, and rough. But careful.
Give it the business. All of it. The works.

And finally the big stuff.
(Make a note of this, must think it all out.)
Stuff about the reason for all the other stuff.
Business about loyalty (the need for, and so forth), brains (stuff,
stuff), and something about the breaks.
Business about what it is that makes the whole business go round
without any beginning and without any end, like the wind
or like the ocean, a feeling to tear the heart out of a wooden
Indian's breast.

Straight stuff. Real stuff. True stuff. The McCoy.
Sometime. Soon. Before it's too late.
Because, after all.
And so on, and so on, and so on, and so on.

And Steve, the athlete, where is he?

And Clark, the medico who played Chopin and quoted Keats, where is he now?

And Dale, who built that bridge (so often shown in the rotogravures) taming a veritable Styx on some fabulous continent?

Elvira, who dealt in nothing less than truths that were absolute?

And Henderson, law student who floated a financial empire, is it true he died in jail?

And true that Steve is bald, and broke, and fat?

And true that Dale's long bridge is a tangle of junk, destroyed by dynamite in a great retreat?

Perhaps the empire of credit was not, after all, so shrewd or bold.

Perhaps Clark did much better in drygoods, to tell the truth, than he would have with surgery or Keats.

Perhaps Dale's bridge was not, really, a towering miracle. Or it may be such miracles are not so important, after all.

It may be Elvira came as close to the thing, with her absolutes, as anyone else. She's the mother of five.

White mice, running mazes in behavior tests, have never displayed more cunning than these, who arrived by such devious routes at such incredible ends.

For it is the end, surely? We knew the story to be working toward an end, and this, then, is in fact the end?

And there is no chance we will be met tonight, or tomorrow night, or any other night, by destiny moving in still another direction?

As one might meet a figure on a dark street, and hear from the shadows a familiar but unwelcome voice:

"Hello, remember me? We had an appointment, but you broke it
    to attend a class reunion.
You can forget that, now. Tonight something new is coming up.
Let's go."

All right, I may have lied to you, and about you, and made a few
      pronouncements a bit too sweeping, perhaps, and possibly
      forgotten to tag the bases here or there,
And damned your extravagance, and maligned your tastes, and
      libeled your relatives, and slandered a few of your friends,
O.K.,
Nevertheless, come back.

Come home. I will agree to forget the statements that you issued
      so copiously to the neighbors and the press,
And you will forget that figment of your imagination, the blonde
      from Detroit;
I will agree that your lady friend who lives above us is not crazy,
      bats, nutty as they come, but on the contrary rather bright,
And you will concede that poor old Steinberg is neither a drunk,
      nor a swindler, but simply a guy, on the eccentric side,
      trying to get along.
(Are you listening, you bitch, and have you got this straight?)

Because I forgive you, yes, for everything,
I forgive you for being beautiful and generous and wise,
I forgive you, to put it simply, for being alive, and pardon you, in
      short, for being you.

Because tonight you are in my hair and eyes,
And every street light that our taxi passes shows me you again,
      still you,
And because tonight all other nights are black, all other hours are
      cold and far away, and now, this minute, the stars are very
      near and bright.

Come back. We will have a celebration to end all celebrations.
We will invite the undertaker who lives beneath us, and a couple
      of the boys from the office, and some other friends,
And Steinberg, who is off the wagon, by the way, and that insane
      woman who lives upstairs, and a few reporters, if anything
      should break.

Now, about that other one, the sober one
(To be objective, for a change, about one's public self. After all,
    each of us has that stupider side),
Yes, you have seen him around, that self-appointed Dr. Jekyll who
    shares (reluctantly) by day this name and being with his
    Mr. Hyde (as he would put it) of the night,

Yes, him,
That fellow with this face, this voice, and even (by some crashing
    magic we will not go into now) possessed with a few of the
    same superficial traits,
That one whose first awakening voice is a hoarse, barbaric blast
    (you know against whom), who damns the excess (how-
    ever moderate), deplores the extravagance and winces (as
    he reaches for the aspirin) at the smallest memory,
That fellow with the curdled eyes and not quite steady hands
    (poor guy, he must be slipping), to say nothing of a disposi-
    tion that is really a wonderful, wonderful thing in itself,

Yes, well, now that you have the picture, take him,
And all his pathetic protests and his monumental vows to abstain,
    totally, forthwith (these need not concern us here)
(Two more of the same)
But, more especially, his pious recantations and denials, his cease-
    less libel of one who is (why dodge the issue?) his mental,
    physical, and yes, moral superior—
But do you begin to see the point?

Because the point is this (he talks of self-respect, and decency is a
    favorite word of his), the point is this:
Does he think that he is the only one?
Does he think that he is the only man on earth who has felt this
    thing?

86

The only person ever to sit and watch the rain drive against the lighted windows, revolving at once some private trouble and knowing, for everything that breathes, a cold impersonal dismay?

From which (drinking, he says, is just an escape) he searches daily, down a thousand familiar avenues, for an escape that simply does not exist
(Those Chinese dreams he palms as reality, those childish ambitions, and then that transparent guile of his),
That fool (who must, it seems, be suffered) (but not gladly), that bore (and who has tolerated most? Has overlooked most? Which of us has forgiven most), that fool in love with some frowsy fate that plays with him as a cat plays with a mouse,
That fool (and this, at last, is the question), what would his decency amount to, but for the simple decency of this escape?

And if this is not true,
If this is not the final truth, then no one here is drunk, drunk as a lord of ancient France,
If this is not the inescapable truth, then the night is not dark but bright as day, and the lights along the street are not really made of burning pearls and rubies dipped in liquid fire,
If this is not true, the truth itself, as hard as hell and stronger than death,
Then time does not fly but life grows younger by the hour, and the rain is not falling, falling, everywhere falling,
And there are not, here, only pleasant sights and sounds and a pleasant warmth.

PAY-OFF

Do you, now, as the news becomes known,
And you have the telegram still in your hand, here in the familiar
    room where there is no sound but the ticking of the clock,
Or there on the street, where you see the first headlines, and it is
    true this time, really true, actual as the green and red of
    the traffic lights, as real as the fruit vendor's rhythmic cry,

Do you recall any being other than this, before your world sud-
    denly shook and settled to this new, strange axis upon
    which it will turn, now, always while you live?
Does it seem possible, now, you were ever bored? Or drunk and
    confident? Or sober and afraid?
Will the sound of the clock ever fade, or the voice of the vendor
    sometime stop?

FIVE A.M.

Street by street the lights go out, and the night turns gray, bring-
　　ing respite to this and to all other agencies,
With the gears of commerce unmeshed and stopped, the channels
　　of communication slowed and stilled
(Radio, ticker, and spirit control)—

Bringing peace, briefly, to the members of the board and bench
　　and staff,
Sleep, for a space, to the journeymen of the switchboard and the
　　dictaphone,
Rest to the lieutenants of steel, and wool, and coal, and wheat,
And to the envoys from abroad (Her Majesty's, His Excellency's,
　　and the mysterious Mr. X),
And to the representatives of the people (both houses), and to the
　　vicars of the Lord (conformist and dissident)
And to the inspectors of the arson, forgery, bomb, and homicide
　　squads—

While the crated shipments of this agency (with those of others)
　　stand in guarded sheds at Quebec,
Wait for release on rainswept wharves of Shanghai and the Rio,
Move, slowly, from a dark siding in Butte.

It is not— I swear it by every fiery omen to be seen these nights in
every quarter of the heavens, I affirm it by all the mon-
strous portents of the earth and of the sea—

It is not that my belief in the true and mystic science is shaken, nor
that I have lost faith in the magic of the cards, or in the
augury of dreams, or in the great and good divinity of the
stars—

No, I know still whose science fits the promise to the inquirer's
need, invariably, for a change: Mine. My science foretells
the wished-for journey, the business adjustment, the hand-
some stranger. (Each of these is considered a decided
change.)

And I know whose skill weighs matrimony, risks a flier in steel or
wheat against the vagaries of the moon—

(Planet of dreams, of mothers and of children, goddess of sailors
and of all adventurers, forgive the liberty. But a man must
eat.) My skill,

Mine, and the cunning and the patience. (Two dollars for the
horoscope in brief and five for a twelve months' forecast in
detail.)

No, it is this: The wonders that I have seen with my own eyes.

It is this: That still these people know, as I do not, that what has
never been on earth before may still well come to pass,

That always, always there are new and brighter things beneath
the sun,

That surely, in bargain basements or in walk-up flats, it must be
so that still from time to time they hear wild angel voices
speak.

It is this: That I have known them for what they are,

Seen thievery written plainly in their planets, found greed and
murder and worse in their birth dates and their numbers,
guilt etched in every line of every palm,

But still a light burns through the eyes they turn to me, a need
more moving than the damned and dirty dollars (which
I must take) that form the pattern of their larger hopes and
deeper fears.

And it comes to this: That always I feel another hand, not mine,
has drawn and turned the card to find some incredible ace,
Always another word I did not write appears in the spirit parch-
ment prepared by me,
Always another face I do not know shows in the dream, the crystal
globe, or the flame.

And finally, this: Corrupt, in a world bankrupt and corrupt, what
have I got to do with these miracles?
If they want miracles, let them consult someone else.
Would they, in extremity, ask them of a physician? Or expect
them, in desperation, of an attorney? Or of a priest? Or of
a poet?

Nevertheless, a man must eat.
Mrs. Raeburn is expected at five. She will communicate with a
number of friends and relatives long deceased.

CONTINUOUS PERFORMANCE

The place seems strange, more strange than ever, and the times
    are still more out of joint;
Perhaps there has been some slight mistake?

It is like arriving at the movies late, as usual, just as the story ends:
There is a carnival on the screen. It is a village in springtime, that
    much is clear. But why has the heroine suddenly slapped
    his face? And what does it mean, the sequence with the
    limousine and the packed valise? Very strange.
Then love wins. Fine. And it is the end. O.K.
But how do we reach that carnival again? And when will that
    springtime we saw return once more? How, and when?

Now, where a moment ago there was a village square, with trees
    and laughter, the story resumes itself in arctic regions
    among blinding snows. How can this be?
What began in the long and shining limousine seems closing now,
    fantastically, in a hansom cab.
The amorous business that ended with happiness forever after is
    starting all over again, this time with a curse and a pistol
    shot. It is not so good.

Nevertheless, though we know it all and cannot be fooled, though
    we know the end and nothing deceives us,
Nevertheless we shall stay and see what it meant, the mystery of
    the packed valise,
Why curses change at last to kisses and to laughter in a limousine
    (for this is fixed, believe me, fixed),
How simply and how swiftly arctic blizzards melt into blowing
    trees and a village fair.

And stay to see the Hydra's head cut off, and grown again, and
    incredibly multiplied,
And observe how Sisyphus fares when he has once more almost
    reached the top,
How Tantalus again will nearly eat and drink.

And learn how Alph the sacred river flows, in Xanadu, forever to
    a sunless sea,
How, from the robes of simple flesh, fate emerges from new and
    always more fantastic fate.

Until again we have the village scene. (And now we know the
    meaning of the packed valise)
And it is a carnival again. In spring.

Recently displayed at the Times Square Station, a new Vandyke
    on the face-cream girl.
(Artist unknown. Has promise, but lacks the brilliance shown by
    the great masters of the Elevated age)
The latest wood carving in a Whelan telephone booth, titled
    "O Mortal Fools WA 9-5090," shows two winged hearts
    above an ace of spades.
(His meaning is not entirely clear, but this man will go far)
A charcoal nude in the rear of Flatbush Ahearn's Bar & Grill,
    "Forward to the Brotherhood of Man," has been boldly
    conceived in the great tradition.
(We need more, much more of this)
Then there is the chalk portrait, on the walls of a waterfront
    warehouse, of a gentleman wearing a derby hat: "Bleecker
    Street Mike is a doublecrossing rat."
(Morbid, but powerful. Don't miss)

Know then by these presents, know all men by these signs and
    omens, by these simple thumbprints on the throat of time,
Know that Pete, the people's artist, is ever watchful,
That Tuxedo Jim has passed among us, and was much displeased,
    as always,
That George the Ghost (no man has ever seen him) and Billy the
    Bicep boy will neither bend nor break,
That Mr. Harkness of Sunnyside still hopes for the best, and has
    not lost his human touch,
That Phantom Phil, the master of them all, has come and gone,
    but will return, and all is well.

CRACKED RECORD BLUES

If you watch it long enough you can see the clock move,
If you try hard enough you can hold a little water in the palm of
    your hand,
If you listen once or twice you know it's not the needle, or the
    tune, but a crack in the record when sometimes a phono-
    graph falters and repeats, and repeats, and repeats, and
    repeats—

And if you think about it long enough, long enough, long enough,
    long enough then everything is simple and you can under-
    stand the times,
You can see for yourself that the Hudson still flows, that the
    seasons change as ever, that love is always love,
Words still have a meaning, still clear and still the same;
You can count upon your fingers that two plus two still equals,
    still equals, still equals, still equals—
There is nothing in this world that should bother the mind.

Because the mind is a common sense affair filled with common
    sense answers to common sense facts,
It can add up, can add up, can add up, can add up earthquakes
    and subtract them from fires,
It can bisect an atom or analyze the planets—
All it has to do is to, do is to, do is to, do is to start at the beginning
    and continue to the end.

There is a jungle, there is a jungle, there is a vast, vivid, wild,
wild, marvelous, marvelous, marvelous jungle,
Open to the public during business hours,
A jungle not very far from an Automat, between a hat store there,
and a radio shop.

There, there, whether it rains, or it snows, or it shines,
Under the hot, blazing, cloudless, tropical neon skies that the
management always arranges there,
Rows and rows of marching ducks, dozens and dozens and dozens
of ducks, move steadily along on smoothly-oiled ballbear-
ing feet,
Ducks as big as telephone books, slow and fearless and out of
this world,
While lines and lines of lions, lions, rabbits, panthers, elephants,
crocodiles, zebras, apes,
Filled with jungle hunger and jungle rage and jungle love,
Stalk their prey on endless, endless rotary belts through never-end-
ing forests, and burning deserts, and limitless veldts,
To the sound of tom-toms, equipped with silencers, beaten by
thousands of savages there.

And there it is that all the big game hunters go, there the traders
and the explorers come,
Leanfaced men with windswept eyes who arrive by streetcar,
auto or subway, taxi or on foot, streetcar or bus,
And they nod, and they say, and they need no more:
"There . . . there . . .
There they come, and there they go."

And weighing machines, in this civilized jungle, will read your
soul like an open book, for a penny at a time, and tell
you all,
There, there, where smoking is permitted,

96

In a jungle that lies, like a rainbow's end, at the very end of every
   trail,
There, in the only jungle in the whole wide world where ducks
   are waiting for streetcars,
And hunters can be psychoanalyzed, while they smoke and wait
   for ducks.

Why do they whistle so loud, when they walk past the graveyard
    late at night?
Why do they look behind them when they reach the gates? Why
    do they have any gates? Why don't they go through the
    wall?
But why, O why do they make that horrible whistling sound?

GO AWAY, LIVE PEOPLE, STOP HAUNTING THE DEAD.

If they catch you, it is said, they make you rap, rap, rap on a
    table all night,
And blow through a trumpet and float around the room in long
    white veils,
While they ask you, and ask you: Can you hear us, Uncle Ted?
Are you happy, Uncle Ted? Should we buy or should we sell?
    Should we marry, Uncle Ted?
What became of Uncle Ned, Uncle Ted, and is he happy, and ask
    him if he knows what became of Uncle Fred?

KEEP AWAY, LIVE PEOPLE, KEEP FAR AWAY,
STAY IN THE WORLD'S OTHER WORLD WHERE YOU REALLY BELONG,
    YOU WILL PROBABLY BE MUCH HAPPIER THERE.

And who knows what they are hunting for, always looking, look-
    ing, looking with sharp bright eyes where they ought to
    have sockets?
Whoever saw them really grin with their teeth?
Who knows why they worry, or what they scheme, with a brain
    where there should be nothing but good, damp air?

STAY AWAY, LIVE PEOPLE, STAY AWAY, STAY AWAY,
YOU MEAN NO HARM, AND WE AREN'T AFRAID OF YOU, AND WE DON'T
    BELIEVE SUCH PEOPLE EXIST,
BUT WHAT ARE YOU LOOKING FOR? WHO DO YOU WANT?
WHO? WHO? WHO? O WHO?

CONFESSION OVERHEARD IN A SUBWAY

You will ask how I came to be eavesdropping, in the first place.
The answer is, I was not.
The man who confessed to these several crimes (call him John
  Doe) spoke into my right ear on a crowded subway train,
  while the man whom he addressed (call him Richard Roe)
  stood at my left.
Thus, I stood between them, and they talked, or sometimes
  shouted, quite literally straight through me.
How could I help but overhear?
Perhaps I might have moved away to some other strap. But the
  aisles were full.
Besides, I felt, for some reason, curious.

"I do not deny my guilt," said John Doe. "My own, first, and after
  that my guilty knowledge of still further guilt.
I have counterfeited often, and successfully.
I have been guilty of ignorance, and talking with conviction. Of
  intolerable wisdom, and keeping silent.
Through carelessness, or cowardice, I have shortened the lives of
  better men. And the name for that is murder.
All my life I have been a receiver of stolen goods."

"Personally, I always mind my own business," said Richard Roe.
  "Sensible people don't get into those scrapes."

I was not the only one who overheard this confession.
Several businessmen, bound for home, and housewives and me-
  chanics, were within easy earshot.
A policeman sitting in front of us did not lift his eyes, at the men-
  tion of murder, from his paper.
Why should I be the one to report these crimes?
You will understand why this letter to your paper is anonymous.
  I will sign it: Public-Spirited Citizen, and hope that it
  cannot be traced.

But all the evidence, if there is any clamor for it, can be substan-
tiated.
I have heard the same confession many times since, in different
places.
And now that I come to think of it, I had heard it many times
before.

"Guilt," said John, "is always and everywhere nothing less than
guilt.
I have always, at all times, been a willing accomplice of the crass
and the crude.
I have overheard, daily, the smallest details of conspiracies against
the human race, vast in their ultimate scope, and conspired,
daily, to launch my own.
You have heard of innocent men who died in the chair. It was
my greed that threw the switch.
I helped, and I do not deny it, to nail that guy to the cross, and
shall continue to help.
Look into my eyes, you can see the guilt.
Look at my face, my hair, my very clothing, you will see guilt
written plainly everywhere.
Guilt of the flesh. Of the soul. Of laughing, when others do not.
Of breathing and eating and sleeping.
I am guilty of what? Of guilt. Guilty of guilt, that is all, and
enough."

Richard Roe looked at his wristwatch and said: "We'll be twenty
minutes late.
After dinner we might take in a show."

Now, who will bring John Doe to justice for his measureless crimes?
I do not, personally, wish to be involved.
Such nakedness of the soul belongs in some other province,
probably the executioner's.

And who will bring the blunt and upright Richard Roe to the
      accuser's stand, where he belongs?
Or will he deny and deny his partnership?

I have done my duty, as a public-spirited citizen, in any case.

KING JUKE

The juke-box has a big square face,
A majestic face, softly glowing with red and green and purple
    lights.
Have you got a face as bright as that?

BUT IT'S A PROVEN FACT, THAT A JUKE-BOX HAS NO EARS.

With its throat of brass, the juke-box eats live nickels raw;
It can turn itself on or shut itself off;
It has no hangovers, knows no regrets, and it never feels the need
    for sleep.
Can you do that?
What can you do that a juke-box can't, and do it ten times better
    than you?

And it hammers at your nerves, and stabs you through the heart,
    and beats upon your soul—
But can you do that to the box?

Its resourceful mind, filled with thoughts that range from love to
    grief, from the gutter to the stars, from pole to pole,
Can seize its thoughts between fingers of steel,
Begin them at the start and follow them through in an orderly
    fashion to the very end.
Can you do that?
And what can you say that a juke-box can't, and say it in a clearer,
    louder voice than yours?
What have you got, a juke-box hasn't got?

Well, a juke-box has no ears, they say.
The box, it is believed, cannot even hear itself.
IT SIMPLY HAS NO EARS AT ALL.

BEWARE

Someone, somewhere, is always starting trouble,
Either a relative, or a drunken friend, or a foreign state.
Trouble it is, trouble it was, trouble it will always be.
Nobody ever leaves well enough alone.

It begins, as a rule, with an innocent face and a trivial remark:
"There are two sides to every question," or "Sign right here, on
    the dotted line,"
But it always ends with a crash of glass and a terrible shout—
No one, no one lets sleeping dragons sleep.

And it never happens, when the doorbell rings, that you find a
    troupe of houris standing on your stoop.
Just the reverse.
So beware of doorbells. (And beware, beware of houris, too)
And you never receive a letter that says: "We enclose, herewith,
    our check for a million."
You know what the letter always says, instead.
So beware of letters. (And anyway, they say, beware of great
    wealth)

Be careful of doorbells, be cautious of telephones, watch out for
    genial strangers, and for ancient friends;
Beware of dotted lines, and mellow cocktails; don't touch letters
    sent specifically to you;
Beware, especially, of innocent remarks;
Beware of everything,
Damn near anything leads to trouble,
Someone is always, always stepping out of line.

ELEGY IN A THEATRICAL WAREHOUSE

They have laid the penthouse scenes away, after a truly phe-
nomenal run,
And taken apart the courtroom, and the bright, shiny office, and
laid them all away with the cabin in the clearing where
the sun slowly rose through a smashing third act,
And the old family mansion on the road above the mill has been
gone a long time,
And the road is gone—
The road that never did lead to any mill at all.

The telephone is gone, the phone that rang and rang, and never
did connect with any other phone,
And the great steel safe where no diamonds ever were,
They have taken down the pictures, portraits of ancestors lost and
unclaimed, that hung on the massive walls,
And taken away the books that reached to the study ceiling,
The rows and rows of books bound in leather and gold with noth-
ing, nothing, nothing inside—

And the bureaus, and the chests, that were empty to the brim,
And the pistols that brought down so many, many curtains with so
many, many blanks—

Almost everything is gone,
Everything that never held a single thing at all.

PIANO TUNER

It is the sound of a cat like no cat ever seen before walking back
    and forth on ivory keys;
No note on this board, however the wires are tightened, can be
    tuned to any other note;
The instrument cannot be played, not correctly,
Not by any players known today, not from the scores and arrange-
    ments that now exist—

Somehow this wire, however strung, always returns a sound with
    an overtone, and always in the overtone the sound of dis-
    tant gunfire can be plainly heard,
Another, however loose or taut, echoes as though to fingers tap-
    ping not music but bulletins despatched from remote time
    and space,
Then there are chords, neither minor chords nor discords, in some
    way filled with a major silence—

And it cannot be, it is not according to the standard scale;
Some wholly new and different kind of scale, perhaps, with un-
    known values, or no values, or values measured by chance
    and change—

This key responds with something not even sound at all, some-
    times a feeling, and the feeling is anguish,
Sometimes a sense, like the touch of a hand,
Or a glimpse of familiar rooftops wrapped first in summer sun-
    light and then in falling snow—

As though the instrument were devil'd by melodies not writ-
    ten yet,
Or possessed by players not yet born.

MODEL FOR A BIOGRAPHY

Years in sporting goods, rich in experience, were followed by
    years in soda, candy, and cigars.
(If there is some connection, you might point it out here)
A real estate venture, resulting in ruin, prepared this man for his
    later triumph in the hardware game.
(If there is no connection, or if the logic seems weak, his is not
    the first life that failed to make sense—
You had better play it safe, and stick to one point):

HE WAS EXPERIENCED. HE WAS PREPARED.

And years of marriage (a happy, happy marriage) prepared him
    for years and years of divorce.
(O happy divorce)
(But you'd better not say that. Think of the relatives. And the
    public, by and large, would not believe you, or if they did,
    would not understand)
Then what can you say? You have to say something that makes
    a little sense:

HE WAS EXPERIENCED. HE WAS PREPARED.

He was kind, without fail, to other people's mothers;
Reprieved from insurance, he was sentenced to a bank, but made
    a daring, spectacular daylight escape;
Rejected by the Marines, he was welcomed by the Quartermaster
    Corps with open arms,
And when it is over, well, when it is over:

HE WILL BE EXPERIENCED. HE WILL BE PREPARED.

END OF THE SEERS' CONVENTION

We were walking and talking on the roof of the world,
In an age that seemed, at that time, an extremely modern age
Considering a merger, last on the agenda, of the Seven Great
    Leagues that held the Seven True Keys to the Seven Ul-
    timate Spheres of all moral, financial, and occult life.

"I foresee a day," said one of the delegates, an astro-analyst from
    Idaho, "when men will fly through the air, and talk across
    space;
They will sail in ships that float beneath the water;
They will emanate shadows of themselves upon a screen, and the
    shadows will move, and talk, and seem as though real."

"Very interesting, indeed," declared a Gypsy delegate.
"But I should like to ask, as a simple reader of tea-leaves and
    palms:
How does this combat the widespread and growing evil of the
    police?"

The astrologer shrugged, and an accidental meteor fell from his
    robes and smoldered on the floor.
"In addition," he said, "I foresee a war,
And a victory after that one, and after the victory, a war again."

"Trite," was the comment of a crystal-gazer from Miami Beach.
"Any damn fool, at any damn time, can visualize wars, and more
    wars, and famines and plagues.
The real question is: How to seize power from entrenched and
    organized men of Common Sense?"

"I foresee a day," said the Idaho astrologer, "when human beings
    will live on top of flag-poles,
And dance, at some profit, for weeks and months without any rest,
And some will die very happily of eating watermelons, and nails,
    and cherry pies."

"Why," said a bored numerologist, reaching for his hat, "can't
these star-gazers keep their feet on the ground?"
"Even if it's true," said a Bombay illusionist, "it is not, like the
rope-trick, altogether practical."

"And furthermore and finally," shouted the astrologer, with
comets and halfmoons dropping from his pockets, and his
agitated sleeves,
"I prophesy an age of triumph for laziness and sleep, and dreams
and utter peace.
I can see couples walking through the public parks in love, and
those who do not are wanted by the sheriff.
I see men fishing beside quiet streams, and those who do not are
pursued by collectors, and plastered with liens."

"This does not tell us how to fight against skepticism," muttered
a puzzled mesmerist, groping for the door.
"I think," agreed a lady who interpreted the cards, "we are all
inclined to accept too much on faith."

A sprinkling of rain, or dragon's blood,
Or a handful of cinders fell on the small, black umbrellas they
raised against the sky.

FINALE

How cold, how very cold is the wind that blows out of nowhere
    into nowhere,
Winding across space and uncalendar'd time,

Filled with the sound of living voices, as it winds through the
    ears that once were Stephen's ears,
Charged with theh scent of fields and forests, as it blows through
    the nostrils that once were Jane's,

Winding through the sockets that once were David's eyes,
Weaving again, as she used to do, the soft brown hair that once
    was Mary's hair,
Bringing again the words that once were Stephen's and David's
    and Mary's words into and out of their deaf ears,
Scattering the worlds that once were theirs, and yours, and mine,
Bearing away to nowhere and to no place the very especial sins
    and virtues that once were ours,

How cold, how extremely cold is this wind.

A TRIBUTE, AND A NIGHTMARE

You wonder, sometimes, but more often worry, and feel dismayed
    in a world of change,
Seeing landmarks vanish, old bastions fall, and you frequently
    question what Fate may have in store for you—
But you really need not—
Whatever else it holds, it holds the changeless and eternal Martin
    Dies.

Will the world be bright, and filled with laughter?
You will hear all about it from Congressman Dies (Chairman of
    the Committee to Investigate Gloom).

Will the world be grim, inhabited by wolves with long, sharp
    teeth?
It will not go unchampioned. See Martin Dies, President of the
    Anti-Grandma League.

Will the people of the earth be nudists, eventually, and largely
    vegetarian?
Be especially wary of Dies, Martin, spinach crusader, the Kiddies'
    Kandidate unanimously acclaimed by Martin Dies.
Will the planet be Red with revolution (you hope) from the
    tropics to the poles?
You will have to deal (you fear, and rightly) with Commissar
    Dies, Chairman of the Committee to Probe Versive Ac-
    tivity.

Stranger, whoever you are, and whatever your final destination
    may be,
I give you, freely, a name to conjure with:
In heaven: Martin Dies, Chairman of the Membership Committee,
In hell: Martin Dies, President of United Coke & Coal.

AFTERNOON OF A PAWNBROKER

Still they bring me diamonds, diamonds, always diamonds,
Why don't they pledge something else for a change, if they must
    have loans, other than those diamond clasps and diamond
    rings,
Rubies, sapphires, emeralds, pearls,
Ermine wraps, silks and satins, solid gold watches and silver plate
    and violins two hundred years old,
And then again diamonds, diamonds, the neighborhood diamonds
    I have seen so many times before, and shall see so many
    times again?

Still I remember the strange afternoon (it was a season of ex-
    traordinary days and nights) when the first of the strange
    customers appeared,
And he waited, politely, while Mrs. Nunzio redeemed her furs,
    then he stepped to the counter and he laid down a thing
    that looked like a trumpet,
In fact, it was a trumpet, not mounted with diamonds, not plated
    with gold or even silver, and I started to say: "We can't
    use trumpets—"
But a light was in his eyes,
And after he was gone, I had the trumpet. And I stored it away.
    And the name on my books was Gabriel.

It should be made clear my accounts are always open to the
    police, I have nothing to conceal,
I belong, myself, to the Sounder Business Principles League,
Have two married daughters, one of them in Brooklyn, the other
    in Cleveland,
And nothing like this had ever happened before.
How can I account for my lapse of mind?
All I can say is, it did not seem strange. Not at the time. Not in
    that neighborhood. And not in that year.

And the next to appear was a man with a soft, persuasive voice,
And a kindly face, and the most honest eyes I have ever seen, and
ears like arrows, and a pointed beard,
And what he said, after Mrs. Case had pledged her diamond ring
and gone, I cannot now entirely recall,
But when he went away I found I had an apple. An apple, just an
apple.
"It's been bitten," I remember that I tried to argue. But he smiled,
and said in his quiet voice: "Yes, but only twice."
And the strangest thing is, it did not seem strange. Not strange
at all.

And still those names are on my books.
And still I see listed, side by side, those incongruous, and not very
sound securities:
(1) Aladdin's lamp (I must have been mad), (1) Pandora's box,
(1) Magic carpet,
(1) Fountain of youth (in good condition), (1) Holy Grail,
(1) Invisible man (the only article never redeemed, and
I cannot locate him), and others, others, many others,
And still I recall how my storage vaults hummed and crackled,
from time to time, or sounded with music, or shot forth
flame,
And I wonder, still, that the season did not seem one of unusual
wonder, not even different—not at the time.

And still I think, at intervals, why didn't I, when the chance was
mine, drink just once from that Fountain of youth?
Why didn't I open that box of Pandora?
And what if Mr. Gabriel, who redeemed his pledge and went
away, should some day decide to blow on his trumpet?
Just one short blast, in the middle of some busy afternoon?

But here comes Mr. Barrington, to pawn his Stradivarius.
And here comes Mrs. Case, to redeem her diamond ring.

112

Not here, but a little farther, after we have passed through the
hall of mirrors,
Seeing ourselves as ogres, devils, zombies, diplomats,
And after we have entered the dragon's jaws, drifting in our
wooden boat down a silent river between white, gaping,
enormous teeth,
Floating in darkness through grottos of ogres, then plastic devils
stoking the painted flames of a gospel hell,
Coming safely again into sunlight, and the sound of a band—

To a cavern of echoes, where we hear the fun as strangers rehearse
and rehearse the surprise they shall give themselves to-
morrow,
Watch the signs flash red, and gold, and blue, and green,
"Eat" "Drink" "Be Merry" "At Mike's,"
Where there is no score, in any game, less than a million magic
bells and a billion electric lights—

Beyond the highest peak of the steepest roller-coaster, in the
company of persons we do not know,
Through arcades where anyone, even hermits can have their for-
tunes told by iron gypsies sealed behind plateglass walls,
Into and beyond the bazaars where every prize is offered, dolls
and vases, clocks and pillows, miniature closets for the
family skeleton,
Given freely, with no questions asked, to any, any winner at all—

Until we emerge, safe at last, upon that broad and crowded beach,
To cry aloud: Is there a stranger here?
The stranger we have come so far, and through so many dangers,
to find?
That one who, alone, can solve these many riddles we have found
so difficult:—

Who, among us all, is the most popular person?
Whom shall we vote the handsomest, the wittiest, most likely to
      succeed?
What is the name, and the mission, of the embryo so long pre-
      served in a jar of alcohol?
How may we ever distinguish between an honest, and a criminal
      face?—

Is this stranger somewhere among you?
Perhaps sprawled beneath a striped umbrella, asleep in the sand,
      or tossing a rubber ball to a child,
Or even now awaiting us, aware of our needs, knowing the very
      day and the hour.

SPOTLIGHT

The hour that was bleak, as he worked, does not betray itself in
    the gem that the craftsman has polished;
Nor do the facets of the stone, however they sparkle, give evidence
    of the hour that, to him, was gay;
The day that was overlong, perhaps because of household de-
    mands, is not apparent here in these swiftly changing lights;
None of this shows at all in the rare thing set in the finished clasp—

Nor is there any hint that the maker was either young, or old;
Whether happily married, or often distraught;
No suggestion that he was concerned, as he cut and ground and
    polished, by the thought of uninvited relatives, or a wel-
    come face;
No clue that he lived in a certain house, on a certain street,
That possibly the neighbors were a nuisance, the street too slov-
    enly, the children a few too many in the daytime and the
    traffic too loud at night—

You, wearing this perfect stone, will have no inkling of these
    things at all;
You will understand that the spotlight, in fact, falls elsewhere;
You, and you alone, will know the hour that is really grim, and
    the truly magic face.

4 A.M.

It is early evening, still, in Honolulu, and in London, now, it must
      be well past dawn,
But here in the Riviera Café, on a street that has been lost and
      forgotten long ago, as the clock moves steadily toward
      closing time,
The spark of life is very low, if it burns at all—

And here we are, four lost and forgotten customers in this place
      that surely will never again be found,
Sitting, at ten-foot intervals, along this lost and forgotten bar
(Wishing the space were further still, for we are still too close
      for comfort),
Knowing that the bartender, and the elk's head, and the picture
      of some forgotten champion
(All gazing at something of interest beyond us and behind us,
      but very far away),
Must somehow be aware of us, too, as we stare at the cold interior
      of our lives reflected in the mirror beneath and in back
      of them—

Hear how lonely the radio is, as its voice talks on and on, unan-
      swered,
How its music proves again that one's life is either too humdrum
      or too exciting, too empty or too full, too this, too that;
Only the cat that has been sleeping in the window, now yawning
      and stretching and trotting to the kitchen to sleep again,
Only this living toy knows what we feel, knows what we are,
      really knows what we merely think we know—

And soon, too soon, it will be closing time, the door will be locked,
Leaving each of us alone, then, with something too ravaging for
      a name
(Our golden, glorious futures, perhaps)—

Lock the door now and put out the lights, before some terrible
    stranger enters and puts, to each of us, a question that must
    be answered with the truth—

They say the Matterhorn at dawn, and the Northern Lights of the
    Arctic, are things that should be seen;
They say, they say—in time, you will hear them say anything, and
    everything;
What would the elk's head, or the remote bartender say, if they
    could speak?
The booth where last night's love affair began, the spot where
    last year's homicide occurred, are empty now, and still.

CASTAWAY

I know your neckties where they line the rack, orderly from day
      to day, from year to year,
And the clothing, except for the suit you wear, unwrinkled on the
      hangers, with each thing perfect in its perfect place—

O CASTAWAY, BEWARE—

You, a trifle anxious in this impersonal place, a little worried in
      these fiery times, but holding securely to your solid reef,
Certain you will arise upon the morning as strong and young as
      you are today—

O CASTAWAY, O CASTAWAY—

Send messages now, press many buttons and make phone calls,
      seek the best advice and speed, speed the telegrams for aid,
You do not want to meet the same fate as those others who have
      been cast out, and cast so far away—

Not one of those marooned here in some quiet office, park, or
      decent hotel,
The dreamers, or those too careful, the silent, or one of those who
      abruptly shouts aloud on some busy street,
Anarchist and time-server, timid and self-assured alike—

Each showing in his eyes, in the way he flexes his fingers, in the
      very way he speaks,
Each proving that he also recalls,
Remembers how the elders were all abandoned here, and knows
      that the young may fail in confusion, too—

Therefore, while the long sun rises, and still there is no sign,
But before the pale sun sets again, and then it will be too late—

O CASTAWAY, O CASTAWAY, O CASTAWAY, BEWARE.

HIGHER MATHEMATICS

So many asteroids speed and flash and spin along the heavenly
　　way where Francis L. Regan travels his regular rounds
(More at ease than you or I would be in a walk to the corner store),
Covering countless light-years in a single, lonely, brave patrol,
Seeking, and being sought by so many departed souls, legendary,
　　half-remembered, or those now wholly lost—

Some of whom will be photographed, in their spectral beings, by
　　Francis L. Regan,
The portraits to be displayed, later, in the window of the Psychic
　　Institute
(Showing both Before, and After),
The spirit resembling the original features, except they are paler
　　and more serene—

But among all these hosts, in so many eons and in so much space,
　　there is only one Mr. Regan,
One photographer to the dead (by self-appointment), whose
　　business hours, for mundane sittings, are from nine to five,
Who has a definite social security number, and whose lodge dues
　　are paid to date,
Whose hobbies, habits, likes and dislikes are not noticeably
　　strange,
Who lives in a solid house on a tangible street—

Whose own earthly presence is limited, no less than yours and
　　mine,
But who could, if today he wished, return from the farthest
　　reaches with a picture of the world's first man.

M.D.

We cough. We shiver. We have seizures of pain, and weakness.
    Often there is blood.
We are not as strong as we thought ourselves to be—

Doctor, we urge you, help us—

Our throats are simply throats, not as good as the least of our am-
    plifiers made of bright and lasting steel,
Our minds are not as swift and sure as the machines that add, sub-
    tract, divide in the twinkling of an eye,
Our eyes themselves are subject to strange fatigues, less discern-
    ing than the many magic eyes that we have made,
There is a certain amount of fear that we ourselves shall never be
    able to compete—

Yes, it is the fear. And also the blood. Always the blood.
No, it is the muscles. Or something in the bones. Perhaps in the
    very heart itself.
If you could see us as we are in the morning, shivering in that
    dread—

Understanding death, but knowing something worse than death
    is there, present in the blood.
Or in the unsteady tendons. Or is it the nerves? The joints.
The teeth. The hair. The clumsy limbs. Perhaps the soul—

We have had so much contact with one another, each has been so
    often exposed to each,
The dangers of this contamination are so very great, so terrible—

O Doctor, Doctor, Doctor—

THE JUKE-BOX SPOKE AND THE
JUKE-BOX SAID:

A few of them, sometimes, choose record number 9,
Or sometimes number 12,
And once in a while someone likes selection 5,
But the voice they really crave, all of them, everywhere and al-
    ways, from the hour the doors open until the hour they
    close,
Repeated and repeated like a beating human heart,
Echoing in the walls, the ceiling, shaking the tables, the chairs,
    the floor—

OVER AND OVER, IT IS SELECTION NUMBER 8—

Whispered and chuckling, as though it arose from the bottom of
    the earth,
Or sometimes exploding like thunder in the room,
Not quite a curse and not exactly a prayer,
Eternally the same, but different, different, different every time—

THE WORDS OF NUMBER 8, THE MELODY OF NUMBER 8, THE SOUL OF
    NUMBER 8

Saying the simple thing they cannot say themselves,
Again and again, voicing the secret that they must reveal, and can
    never tell enough,
Yet it never quite gets told—

Sometimes number 9, or 12,
Or 5—

BUT ALWAYS NUMBER 8, AND ONCE AGAIN NUMBER 8,
TIME AFTER TIME, JUST ONCE MORE NUMBER 8 . . . 8 . . . 8 . . .

LANISTA

Behold the afternoon sun, how slowly it withdraws from the sand,
    those darker stains within the shadows, though they have
    been covered and covered again, growing darker still,
Behold the stone tiers, how empty now,
Behold this day, merely a day, but rumored it may be the last on
    which these simple games, our great sports are ever held—

I, Arius, trainer of the best, matched in my youth against the best,
And against them all,
The swordsmen of every province, the netmen, even the beasts—

Knowing no mother or father save this arena, and no other life,
Twenty-eight killed (more than fifty palms), four times spared
    (once by the Emperor, saved by the people thrice),
Sometimes still seeing my portrait on the lamps, the vases, the
    matrons' gems
(In addition to the jeweled chains, the helmets, purses, and other
    favors once given me),
And my name, that I have heard in song—

And knowing as well a certain midnight of the spirit that comes to
    all, when each, in his cell, must be chained against self-
    destruction,
Only to be scourged on the very next day, by whips and red-hot
    irons, to the dangerous fight—

Yet now I hear, with wonder, that none of this has been of any
    avail,
These combats have had no meaning and are in fact nothing, less
    than nothing at all—

As though the fight between the women and the dwarfs had been
    for nothing,
And the combat between the crippled and the blind, had that
    no point?
Is it not good that the race shall ever behold itself with pride and
    disgust, horror and fright?—

So they say this may be the last of our little games—

Well,
We shall see.

NEWSPAPERMAN

This charge was laid upon me long ago: Do not forget;
Remember these lives, that the world in turn will not forget—

Big John Marino, the terror of his district,
Where none were as strong as he, none as handsome, as cunning,
    as cruel,
Saying, before the state destroyed him:
"Tell them the truth. Tell them everything, so they will always
    know."
Know always, therefore, the great, the ruthless and bold, the one
    and only Big John—

Do not forget the fabulous bankrupt, and the vivid fortunes that
    somewhere, surely, the years still guard;
Keep the memory of an heiress, flashlit favorite in a season that
    cannot fade;
Never let fade, altogether, the programs identifying those others,
    miscellaneous members of the cast—

Each of them unique, though now the names, faces, and stories
    are obscured,
Each saying in words, or underneath the words, and some with
    their sealed eyes and cold lips
(But even so they were sure of themselves, still sure)
Urging always: "It is vital;
You must remember the fateful beginning, fully to understand
    the end
(Though of course there can be no real end);
To grasp the motives, fully, it is vital to remember the stamp of
    the mind,
Vital to know even the twist of the mind. . . ."

You will remember me?
Do not forget a newspaperman who kept his word.

Every need analyzed, each personal problem weighed, carefully,
      and solved according to the circumstance of each
(No investment too great. No question too small)
In confidence, at no cost, embarrassment, or obligation to you—

Offering maximum safety
(At 5%)
Full protection against change and chance, rust, moths, and the
      erratic flesh
(Trusts in perpetuity. Impartial executors of long-range wills)
Year after year, security in spite of the treacherous currents of
      impulse, yours and others',
Despite the swiftest tide of affairs—

Rails, chemicals, utilities, steel,
Listed or unlisted, let these stand guard through the shadowy
      times to be,
The heavy parchment with its exact phrases proof you shall walk
      this day's path, identically, tomorrow,
That as long as you wish you may see these streets and parks with
      the same eyes,
The same mood as today—

As though your features, yours, were stamped on the wind, yet
      more lasting than bronze,
The voice, free as always, yet recorded forever,
Your being, yours, still with its problems stronger than even the
      chemicals or the steel—

Decades of experience behind each portfolio can protect that
      future,
Filled with its unfinished business, incomplete desire, and still
      with the stubborn will to protect that future—

All of this, plus 5% of this, until the end of time.

SHERLOCK SPENDS A DAY IN THE COUNTRY

The crime, if there was a crime, has not been reported as yet;
The plot, if that is what it was, is still a secret somewhere in this
    wilderness of newly fallen snow;
The conference, if it was a conference, has been adjourned, and
    now there is nothing in this scene but pine trees, and si-
    lence, and snow, and still more snow.

Nevertheless, in spite of all this apparent emptiness, notice the
    snow;
Observe how it literally crawls with a hundred different signa-
    tures of unmistakable life.
Here is a delicate, exactly repeated pattern, where, seemingly, a
    cobweb came and went,
And here some party, perhaps an acrobat, walked through these
    woods at midnight on his mittened hands.
Thimbles, and dice tracks, and half moons, these trademarks lead
    everywhere into the hills;
The signs prove some amazing fellow on a bicycle rode straight
    up the face of a twenty-foot drift,
And someone, it does not matter who, walked steadily somewhere
    on obviously cloven feet.

Let us ourselves adjourn to the village bar, Watson (not saying
    very much when we get there),
To consider this mighty, diversified army, and what grand con-
    spiracy of conspiracies it hatched,
What conclusions it reached, and where it intends to strike, and
    when,
Being careful to notice, as we go and return, the character and
    number of our own tracks in the snow.

MRS. FANCHIER AT THE MOVIES

If I could reply, but once, to these many new and kindly com-
    panions I have found
(Now that so many of the old are gone, so far and for so long)
Overhearing them on the radio or the phonograph, or here in the
    motion pictures, as now—

These electrical voices, so sure in the sympathy they extend,
Offering it richly through the long hours of the day and the longer
    hours of the night
(Closer at hand, and although automatic, somehow more under-
    standing than a live friend)
Speaking sometimes to each other, but often straight at me—

Wishing I could reply, if only once,
Add somehow to the final burst of triumphant music, or even in
    tragedy mingle with the promise of the fading clouds—

But wondering, too, what it really was I at one time felt so
    deeply for,
The actual voice, or this muted thunder? These giant shadows, or
    the naked face?
Or something within the voice and behind the face?—

And wondering whether, now, I would have the courage to reply,
    in fact,
Or any longer know the words, or even find the voice.

THE FACE IN THE BAR ROOM MIRROR

Fifteen gentlemen in fifteen overcoats and fifteen hats holding
    fifteen glasses in fifteen hands,
Staring and staring at fifteen faces reflected in the mirror behind
    the polished bar,
Tonight, as last night,
And the night before that, and night after night, after night, after
    night—

What are they dreaming of,
Why do they come here and when will it happen, that thing for
    which they return and return,
To stand and wait, and wait, and wait, and wait—

What fifteen resolves are growing clear and hard, between cryptic
    remarks, in those fifteen living silences,
What crystal stairs do they climb or descend into fifteen unseen
    heavens or hells,
What fifteen replies do they give the single question, does any-
    thing on earth ever change, or stay?—

Before the shot rings out, the mirror shatters, the floor gapes open
    and the heavens fall,
And they go at last on their fifteen separate, purposeful ways—

Fifteen magicians,
Masters of escape from handcuff and rope, straitjacket, padlock,
    dungeon and chain,
Now planning escapes still more dazzling,
And fifteen times more terrible than these.

THE PEOPLE V. THE PEOPLE

I have never seen him, this invisible member of the panel, this
    thirteenth juror, but I have certain clues;
I know, after so many years of practice, though I cannot prove
    I know;
It is enough to say, I know that I know.

He is five feet nine or ten, with piercing, bright, triumphant eyes;
He needs glasses, which he will not wear, and he is almost cer-
    tainly stone deaf.
(Cf. Blair v. Gregg, which he utterly ruined.)
He is the juror forever looking out of the window, secretly smiling,
    when you make your telling point.
The one who is wide awake when you think he is asleep. The man
    who naps with his eyes wide open.
Those same triumphant eyes.
He is the man who knows. And knows that he knows.

His hair is meager and he wears wash ties, but these are not im-
    portant points.
He likes the legal atmosphere, that is plain, because he is always
    there.
It is the decent, the orderly procedure that he likes.
He is the juror who arrived first, though you thought he was late;
    the one who failed to return from lunch, though you had
    not noticed.
Let me put it like this: He is the cause of your vague uneasiness
    when you glance about and see that the other twelve are
    all right.

I would know him if I were to see him, I could swear to his
    identity, if I actually saw him once;
I nearly overheard him, when I was for the defense: "They never
    indict anyone unless they are guilty;"

And when I was the State: "A poor man (or a rich man) doesn't
    stand a chance."
Always, before the trial's end, he wants to know if the sergeant
    knew the moon was full on that particular night.

And none of this matters, except I am convinced he is the unseen
    juror bribed, bought, and planted by The People,
An enemy of reason and precedent, a friend of illogic,
Something, I now know, that I know that I really know—

And he or anyone else is welcome to my Blackstone, or my
    crowded shelves of standard books,
In exchange for the monumental works I am convinced he has
    been writing through the years:
"The Rules of Hearsay;" "The Laws of Rumor;"
"An Omnibus Guide to Chance and Superstition," by One Who
    Knows.

ELEGY

Cherubs of stone, smiling, wait and watch above the grave of the
Greenpoint child,
Arrowheads still lie at his hand, ready to serve the Dakota man,
and bowls to refresh him after the long hunt,
Trusted sentinels, open-eyed and leaning on their spears, stand
guard before the airless tomb of the immortal King of
Egypt, Lord of the earth, favorite of the heavens—

But who still watch those very sparks that once arose at midnight
from that fire, there beside the river's edge,
What now serves the resolve, molded in fever, taken by one who
for the first time saw and measured the city's walls,
Who knows the gesture that brought a moment's laughter to one,
alone, who caught it then on a crowded street—

And when will the King arise from his prolonged rest, to pursue
the ancient enemy in his chariot once more,
When will the hunter again return from the chase, to seize his
bowl,
When will the Greenpoint child once more go out, and attend
to his serious play in the sun?

And now you see the artificial sun come up, everywhere suffusing
    a marvelously painted sky;
It is dawn, revealing leagues of earth, and a taxidermist's frozen
    version of the actual life—

There is the Executive in his office; he is serious, but pleasant; a
    man of great importance in and to his day
(See the telephone? And the ashtray and the desk pad, to the very
    life);
Here is the smiling Junior Clerk; the Typist;
And that one is the Salesman, laughing as he seems about to light
    a fresh cigar—

HABITAT: N. AMERICA, it says,
And as the light grows clear and gold, there are the bridges,
    towers, railways, docks
(Exactly scaled to one one-thousandth size, it says),
And there a tiny crane unloads a perfect ship—

The activity increases (for the day, too, is only one one-thousandth
    size);
A ticker races, and soon, very soon, a bell will ring;
See the mail truck leave with letters bound for the utmost horizons
    of this empire limited only by the telephone, the radio,
    and the mail;
In a moment, that toy elevator will reach the top; a signal block
    will fall;
And pretty soon, there will be a silvery bell—

In those adjoining rooms, likewise equipped with phones and
    desks and miniature lights
(The scene is indescribably real, and this is a gay, casual little
    tableau),
Sit the Switchboard Girl, the jovial Attorney—
But there is the bell—success, success—

And we must go, for there is still so much to see in a single after-
noon;
All the exhibits that follow this: the Second Age of Innocence,
the Era of the Torrents, the Third Age of Fire—

But before we leave we must watch the measured sun go down,
and see the miniature trains light up,
Winding their way through moonlit hills toward distant cities that
we know are blazing with lights, with electric signs where
giants walk and mermaids swim—

Knowing, also, that somewhere in the darkness behind us the
Typist is still busily polishing her fingernails,
The Executive, though the office is darkened, is still poised for
action, and the laughing Salesman still clings to his long
cigar,
Each of them comfortable and secure as in life, each mulling some
personal problem,
Each confidently waiting for the sun that will surely rise.

MINUTES FROM THE CHAMBER OF COMMERCE

Ten divisions of bacillus Z stand poised at strategic points along
the last frontier,
Fully trained and equipped,
And we face the future with confidence—

PROVIDED THE FUTURE DOES NOT COME TODAY—

Another vintage ancestor has been dug up in Crete, thirty ruined
cities beneath the ruins on top,
The archeologists are digging, still,
And we in this city are prepared to take whatever fate may offer—

PROVIDED THE OFFER IS SOUND—

We know that voice-recorders have been attached to the phones
of certain business rivals,
We have heard a rumor there may be thought-recorders, too,
Whatever the facts, we look them squarely, calmly, soberly in the
face—

BUT ONLY WITH A TALL, COLD DRINK OF RYE IN HAND.

Now, in this moment that has no identical twin throughout all
    time,
Being yours, yours alone,
Intimate as the code engraved upon your fingertips, and as rare—

Marked as your own features, personal as the voice in which you
    conduct your daily affairs,
Complex as those affairs, growing always into a new and still more
    special crisis
(In each of which you have your particular skill at reading the
    omens and the signs),
Here, in this natural scene, in a numbered house on a street with
    a name—

Unique as the signature you find upon some letter you had long
    ago forgotten and mislaid,
Elusive as the mood that letter now recalls, the story and its end
    as briefly alive,
And now as wholly lost—

As though this long but crowded day, itself, could sometime fade,
Had in fact already slipped through the fingers and now were
    gone, gone, simply gone—

Leaving no one, least of all yourself, to enact the unfinished drama
    that you, alone, once knew so well,
No one to complete the triumph, to understand or even believe
    in the disaster that must be repaired,
No one to glimpse this plan that seemed, at one time, must, must,
    must be fulfilled.

LONG JOURNEY

With us, on this journey that begins in the green and chilly sub-
  urbs on a late Spring afternoon
(Rain streaking the windows of the bus)
And in addition to the passengers, the driver confidently seated
  at the wheel—

Goes Captain Wonder of "Macabre Comics," silently plunging
  through infinities of time and space, changing at will from
  man to God
(The young and cynical student of this magic, though spellbound,
  does not really believe)
Everywhere combating evil, at all times fearless, and never, for
  very long, deceived—

While an immortal of the diamond once more rounds third base
  for home,
Jogging easily at the side of one who hears neither the wet tires
  nor the exhaust,
Only the roar of thousands across a sunswept field—

And this, for another, is not an abandoned development we are
  passing now,
A place of ruined mansions and bypassed factories,
It is a giant hall of radio, filled with the instant laughter that
  follows every perfect response—

And now for a moment the sun comes out, on this journey that is
  part of a farther voyage still
(Long, long after Magellan)
With the home port long since forgotten, and the ultimate reaches
  not even guessed—

Then a flurry of snow, and after that night, and the last stop
(It is the ten thousandth trip, but no band is playing; there had
      been no champagne at the first)
The driver simply reverses his illumined signs,
Singly, the passengers descend and resume, resume their separate
      ways—

Disillusioned (and used to it), alone and self-absorbed,
Unaware that Sinbad the Sailor has descended with them, and
      that Cyclops, Cinderella, the Princess of the Diamond Isles
      in love with Captain Wonder,
And Jack the Giant Killer have all been companions of theirs—

And that each of these has still a long, much longer way to go.

FAMILY ALBUM (I)

The Pioneers

They lived with dangers they alone could see,
Aware of them, everywhere and always, with X-ray eyes for the
      graver and subtle risks of impending evil and future guilt,
Sorcerers of the newsroom, genii of the wide screen, brevet phre-
      nologists of bureau, cabinet, and court,
Consultant wizards of the high, the low, and the middle mirage—

Our forbears, quaint and queer in these posed photographs, stiffly
      smiling, no hint of their martyrdom revealed,
(But for the diaries they commissioned, we would not know their
      heartaches, even now)—

Visionaries (but practical), when the guilty fled in long black
      limousines,
Found clever refuge in opera boxes, night clubs, art galleries and
      public parks,
Our elders pursued in 300 horsepower sportscars, disguised as
      playboys, undercover girls,
If the crisis required it, posed successfully as double or triple
      agents, maniacs, drunks—

For thus they freed that raw, mid-century chaos of little empires
      from the pestilence of false thought;
Helped write, and signed, so many of the Magna Cartas in use to
      this very day;
Issued the first crude registry of licenced Truth;
Sought (and received) patents for the better types of logic,
      durable humour, authentic taste;
Chartered the standard modes of legal prayer, for lease on a yearly
      basis,
(Renewable, with the forms filled in and the stamps affixed, for a
      nominal fee;
This trifling charge scarcely covers the cost;
What matters, of course, is the thought)—

138

God sometimes spoke to them on sleepless nights (as they told us,
        often), and they took down every word,
Revised and edited the counsel in the morning, making sure the
        names and addresses were correct,
Then gave it to the world, stamped: *For Immediate Release—*

They were not Gods, nor did they claim to be;
They were human, and fallible, content to be just what they were:
God's public relations.

FAMILY ALBUM (2)

Granny

This is Grandmother Susan, in one of the few pictures taken by
    the press,
(*Think!* published this one, and here Grandma is leaving court,
    perhaps to gather evidence for the next case)
She is twenty-five, here, in a frock typical of those innocent but
    turbulent times,
And we cannot tell, from the picture, whether she is armed—

Armed and equipped to perfection with the weapon she gave the
    sorcery of her special art,
The recorder snuggled in its holster, the holster concealed in her
    handbag, her girdle, sometimes her brassiere,
(With the listening microphone hidden—where?
The guilty, for all their cunning, never dreamed)
While the steadily turning reels, winding in compact silence,
    caught every guilty nuance of every guilty phrase,
("How about it, babe?" reorganized Chemosene; a drug firm
    failed on a whisper)
Stored away the convincing background noise of ice in shakers,
    the sound of authentic laughter,
And trapped, beyond reasonable doubt, the blackest crimes ever
    committed in speech—

While Granny smiled and dimpled in sympathy:
"Hi-Fi Sue Scores Again,"
"*Think!* names this average, all-round girl America's sweetheart
    of the year"—

Though there were rumours, and slanders, and yes, many jokes;
Grandpa, they said, was a deafmute—

But where are these jokers now?

The Boat

Our scholars say of this latest find, the boat uncovered in the
    desert sands,
Distant from templed places, far from trade routes, remote from
    the sea,
(But seaworthy, preserved in its arid tomb, still perfect in every
    wrought detail)—

They claim that this one, too, is a funeral vessel, designed for
    passage throughout the farthest islands in the sky of death,
Not a landlocked memorial, merely, bound nowhere,
But a solar craft on phantom course (as the helm is fixed) for the
    royal ports of the Ptolemaic year,
Bearing the illustrious dead, in safety, everywhere about that
    planned and prudent empire of the dead,
Under orders sealed by monarchs centuries before, on errands of
    state the dead must observe—

And this accords, it is true, with the intricate innocence of that age,
For they reveled, as we know, in matters that were skilfully and
    lucidly deranged—

But some of our savants claim this boat is of later origin—indeed,
    very late;
These say it derives from a wholly different rite;
This bark, they say, was a test and trial of the atom's might as
    related, mystically, to the actual sea;
That the Idaho ship is not pagan, at all, and differs, in many
    ways, from that early vessel of the Nile.

FAMILY ALBUM (4)

The Investigators

WHO DO YOU, WHO DO YOU, WHO DO YOU, WHO?
WHO DO YOU KNOW, WHO DO YOU HEAR ABOUT, WHO DO YOU SEE AND
    MEET IN YOUR DREAMS AND DAYDREAMS?—

Look what we found when we almost caught him, and he nearly
    confessed again and again,
Stacks and heaps of flagons and flasks and tubes and coils,
"Secret" it says on the door,
(Whatever that means, whoever lost it here, or threw it away, or
    he just forgot)
Crystals and powders and serums and herbs, who's got a hairpin,
Where's a corkscrew,
How would the blue stuff go with a gallon of green?—

WHO, WHO, WHO?
WHAT WERE YOU WHEN, WHY WERE YOU WHAT, WHERE WERE YOU
    WHICH, EITHER HOW OR WHY?

Could it be, no doubt an alchemist lived here once,
(Whoever knows how, it's easy to transmute lead into pure, solid,
    genuine gold)
But why does it look so tasty,
Perhaps you don't rub it on, you drink it instead,
It must be the essence of eternal youth and truth, beauty and
    health and duty and wealth,
Or at least second sight,
What are we waiting for, how will we ever find out until some-
    body tries?—

WHERE DO YOU, WHEN DO YOU?
HOW DO YOU WHICH?
WHO'S IN IT FOR WHAT, WHAT'S IN IT FOR WHO?—

Close your eyes tight, turn around three times, reach and pour and
    stir,
(It says in the rules, one wish per man)
Whatever it is, this is bound to be something final and big,
Open the valve, who's got a match?—

HOW DO YOU, WHEN DO YOU, WHERE DO YOU WHAT?
WHO DO YOU WHO, WHO DO YOU WHO, WHO DO YOU WHO?

DATE DUE